Beginning Xamarin Development for the Mac

Create iOS, watchOS, and Apple tvOS apps
with Xamarin.iOS and Visual Studio for Mac

Dawid Borycki

Apress®

Beginning Xamarin Development for the Mac

Dawid Borycki
Institute of Physical Chemistry,
Polish Academy of Sciences,
Kasprzaka 44/52, Warsaw, 01-224, Poland

ISBN 978-1-4842-3131-9   ISBN 978-1-4842-3132-6 (eBook)
https://doi.org/10.1007/978-1-4842-3132-6

Library of Congress Control Number: 2017963095

Cover image designed by Freepik

Managing Director: Welmoed Spahr
Editorial Director: Todd Green
Acquisitions Editor: Joan Murray
Development Editor: Laura Berendson
Technical Reviewer: Chaim Krause
Coordinating Editor: Jill Balzano
Copy Editor: April Rondeau
Compositor: SPi Global
Indexer: SPi Global
Artist: SPi Global

Distributed to the book trade worldwide by Springer Science+Business Media New York, 233 Spring Street, 6th Floor, New York, NY 10013. Phone 1-800-SPRINGER, fax (201) 348-4505, e-mail orders-ny@springer-sbm.com, or visit www.springeronline.com. Apress Media, LLC is a California LLC and the sole member (owner) is Springer Science + Business Media Finance Inc (SSBM Finance Inc). SSBM Finance Inc is a **Delaware** corporation.

For information on translations, please e-mail rights@apress.com, or visit http://www.apress.com/rights-permissions.

Apress titles may be purchased in bulk for academic, corporate, or promotional use. eBook versions and licenses are also available for most titles. For more information, reference our Print and eBook Bulk Sales web page at http://www.apress.com/bulk-sales.

Any source code or other supplementary material referenced by the author in this book is available to readers on GitHub via the book's product page, located at www.apress.com/9781484231319. For more detailed information, please visit http://www.apress.com/source-code.

Printed on acid-free paper

This book is dedicated to my wife, Agnieszka, daughter, Susanna, and son, Xavier, with love.

We all have dreams. But in order to make dreams come into reality, it takes an awful lot of determination, dedication, self-discipline, and effort.

—Jesse Owens

Contents

About the Author

Dawid Borycki is a software engineer, biomedical researcher, and an expert in several Microsoft developer technologies. He has resolved a broad range of software development challenges for device prototypes (mainly medical equipment), embedded device interfacing, and desktop and mobile programming. Dawid regularly speaks at international developers conferences and has published, cited, and presented on numerous developer topics, including web technologies, mobile/cross-platform development, wearables, embedded, and more.

About the Technical Reviewer

Chaim Krause is an expert computer programmer with over thirty years of experience to prove it. He worked as a lead tech support engineer for ISPs as early as 1995 and as a senior developer support engineer with Borland for Delphi, and has worked in Silicon Valley for over a decade in various roles, including technical support engineer and developer support engineer. He is currently a military simulation specialist for the US Army's Command and General Staff College, working on projects such as developing serious games for use in training exercises. He has also authored several video training courses on Linux topics and has been a technical reviewer for over twenty books, including *iOS Code Testing*, *Android Apps for Absolute Beginners* (4th ed.), and *XML Essentials for C# and .NET Development* (all Apress). It seems only natural then that he would be an avid gamer and have his own electronics lab and server room in his basement. He currently resides in Leavenworth, Kansas, with his loving partner, Ivana, and a menagerie of four-legged companions: their two dogs, Dasher and Minnie, and their three cats, Pudems, Talyn, and Alaska.

Acknowledgments

Dear reader, you hold or view this book thanks to Joan Murray, who was very encouraging of my book proposal and provided a lot of writing tips.

I am grateful to Chaim Krause for providing a very detailed technical review and catching even the smallest mistakes.

Many thanks go to Laura Berendson for reading the manuscript, providing feedback, and giving general advice. I thank Jill Balzano for her patience and keeping track of the book project. I also thank Welmoed Spahr and Todd Green for publishing this book and April Rondeau for copyediting.

Finally, special thanks go to my wife, Agnieszka, daughter, Susanna, and son, Xavier, for their continuous support and patience shown to me during the writing of this book.

Introduction

The programming of mobile apps has recently become one of the most important and exciting aspects of the IT market, leading to numerous applications. At the same time, mobile development is very challenging because of market fragmentation, which is manifested by the presence of devices of different sizes, operating systems, and software development tools. So, to start doing mobile development, you need to take into account these various factors and decide your strategy.

There are three leading mobile platforms: Apple (including iOS, watchOS, and tvOS), Android, and Universal Windows Platform (UWP), each of which provides dedicated tools for developing apps. Each platform has specific hardware requirements. Clearly, iOS SDKs require you to use the local Mac machine or the remote build agent installed on a Mac. UWP apps can be built on Windows 10 machines. Finally, you can use either Mac or Windows machines to develop Android apps. So, first and foremost, the question to answer is that of which hardware to choose. For mobile development, the Intel-based Mac platform is the best choice because it allows you to use macOS and Windows 10 concurrently. The latter can be installed natively through the Boot Camp or virtually using the Parallels Desktop. Accordingly, Mac machines will give you the most flexibility.

After choosing the hardware, you need to select the software development strategy. You have three traditional options here:

- Native apps – In this case, you use platform SDKs, which require you to utilize platform-specific IDEs and programming languages. For instance, in terms of iOS, watchOS, and tvOS, you would need to use either Swift or Objective-C along with Xcode. Native tools give you full access to the platform API at the cost of needing to learn platform-specific programming languages.

- Hybrid apps – They are programmed with web technologies as web pages. These pages are then rendered with a native WebView component, which can be virtually understood as the local web browser, delivered by each platform. In this case, you have a lot of flexibility in terms of programming tools and can use the same code across various platforms at the cost of reduced access to platform-specific APIs.

- Mobile web apps – They are web apps whose views are tailored to mobile devices. Such a strategy is the simplest to apply but does not let you access device components, and it also requires a network connection.

Of course, development strategy is dictated by a number of factors, ranging from your programming preferences to application complexity and target platforms. If you intend to target multiple platforms at the same time, you can choose one of the cross-platform mobile tools, like Xamarin.Forms, Qt Mobile, Embarcadero RAD Studio, or React Native. They provide an additional layer of the unified, platform-independent programming API, which is translated to a platform-specific API during compilation. Importantly, cross-platform instruments provide not only access to the API but also to visual controls. For instance, if you create a message dialog, it will be converted during compilation to the platform-specific message dialog. As a result, in such a "Write once, run anywhere (WORA)" approach, you can indeed compile the same code across various platforms at the cost of flexibility. Finally, if your goal is to extensively utilize platform-specific APIs, you will choose Xamarin.iOS or Xamarin.Android. These let you develop native apps with C# or F#. Xamarin.iOS and Xamarin.Android provide an additional thin layer that maps C# or F# code onto the native platform API. You typically use Xamarin.iOS and Xamarin.Android to implement logic and design the UI separately for each platform. Although you have the extra work of creating platform-specific UIs, you can still share the platform-independent code between various apps. Such an approach gives you two important advantages:

- Your app is native. So, it looks like any other built-in app, as it utilizes native visual controls.

- Your app is written in modern programming language. As a result, you have easy access to numerous libraries and a wide community. This is especially important when you are C# programmer who wants to start developing mobile apps.

In this book, we will learn how to use Xamarin.iOS to develop apps for Apple devices: iPhone and iPad (iOS), Apple Watch (watchOS), and Apple TV (tvOS). We will first prepare the development tools (Visual Studio for Mac) and will get to know available project templates (Chapter 1). Subsequently, I will explicitly show how Xamarin.iOS is related to the native SDKs delivered by Apple, and we will investigate the app structure and lifecycle (Chapter 2). Then, we will learn how to create views (Chapter 3) and implement navigation between them (Chapter 4). Afterward, we will work with touch gestures (Chapter 5), study how to achieve high-quality apps with automatic testing (Chapter 6), and consume data from RESTful web services (Chapter 7). Finally, we will learn how to develop apps for Apple Watches (Chapter 8) and Apple TVs (Chapter 9).

In this book, however, we will not learn how to reuse code between various platforms nor how to develop WORA apps with Xamarin.Forms. You can find more information about this in this book *Beginning Visual Studio for Mac: Build Cross-Platform Apps with Xamarin and .NET Core* by Alessandro Del Sole.

CHAPTER 1

■ ■ ■

Fundamentals

In this chapter, I will guide you through the installation of the development tools you will need for this book. Specifically, we will install Visual Studio for Mac as well as Xcode. The latter is the native toolset for Mac developers. It delivers IDE, SDKs, and also the device simulators we will use. If you have these tools already installed, you can skip to the subsequent section.

After ensuring that all tools are ready, we will create the first Xamarin.iOS app for the iPhone and iPad. This app, shown in Figure 1-1, displays various alerts and responds to user actions. I will also discuss the available project templates that are delivered by Visual Studio. The same templates are available in Xcode, so Xamarin.iOS and Visual Studio let you access iOS platform–specific programming interfaces in a way similar to native development tools but with the ease and smoothness provided by the C# programming language. In this chapter, I will also discuss the basic aspects of designing user interfaces in Visual Studio and show you how to associate event handlers with events fired by visual controls.

■ **Note** In this chapter, I will not discuss Visual Studio for Mac in detail. I will only discuss the necessary elements of this IDE. You can find a comprehensive description of Visual Studio for Mac in the book *Beginning Visual Studio for Mac. Build Cross-Platform Apps with Xamarin and .NET Core* by Alessandro Del Sole.

© Dawid Borycki 2018
D. Borycki, *Beginning Xamarin Development for the Mac*, https://doi.org/10.1007/978-1-4842-3132-6_1

Figure 1-1. *The Hello, World! app we will build in this chapter. The app is executed in the iPhone X simulator.*

Setting Up the Development Environment

To install Visual Studio for Mac, you'll need a Mac with macOS Sierra 10.12 or above. Here, I'll be using either a MacBook Pro or iMac with macOS Sierra 10.16. Once you know that you meet basic platform requirements, you can download the Visual Studio installer from the following website: `http://bit.ly/vs-mac`. Once you have downloaded the installation package, run the installer. A window appears, as shown in Figure 1-2. In this window, you double-click the icon with a down arrow. Subsequently, you will see a dialog informing you that the installer was downloaded from the internet (Figure 1-3). Click the *Open* button to continue.

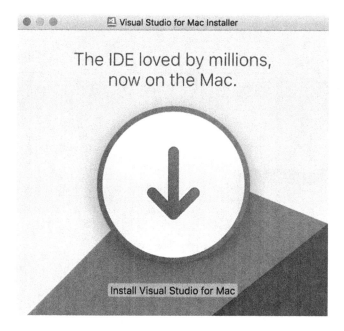

Figure 1-2. *An installer for Visual Studio for Mac*

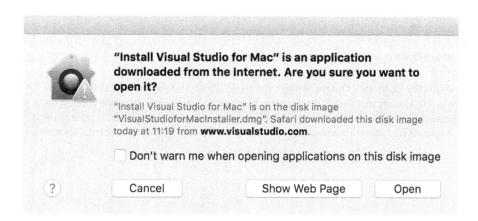

Figure 1-3. *A confirmation dialog*

Visual Studio installer will now verify your system configuration (Figure 1-4). More specifically, it looks for installed components (like Mono Framework, Java SDK, and so on) in order to verify which of them have to be downloaded and installed. Once this is done, another dialog appears on top of the window shown in Figure 1-4. Its header tells you "Thank you for downloading Visual Studio." In this dialog, you simply press the *Continue* button.

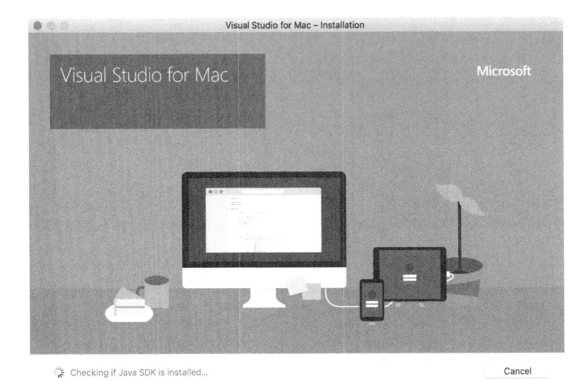

Figure 1-4. *Visual Studio installer is inspecting the operating system*

At this point, the Visual Studio installer might prompt you to install Xcode (Figure 1-5). This happens only if you do not have Xcode already installed. According to this dialog, you can install Xcode concurrently with the Visual Studio installation. Note that the Xcode installation is optional and depends on your current system configuration. I assume that you start with a clean install of macOS and therefore explicitly show how to install Xcode.

Visual Studio for Mac – Installation

Some features require Xcode®

Features like iOS apps and version control require Xcode developer software from Apple®.
You can get Xcode in parallel, so everything is ready by the time the installation is done.

Get Xcode

Cancel   Continue

Figure 1-5. *A dialog prompting for Xcode installation*

To install Xcode, you can press the *Get Xcode* button shown in Figure 1-5. This will direct you to a website, where you click the *View in Mac App Store or Install App* button. It opens the Xcode page in the App Store, on which you only need to click the *Install App* button (Figure 1-6). Alternatively, to install Xcode you can open the Mac App Store locally and then look up Xcode. Irrespective of which method you choose, Xcode and all related developer tools will be downloaded and installed in the background. So, you can now go back to Visual Studio installer.

Figure 1-6. Xcode page in the Mac App Store

The Visual Studio installer will now let you choose which components to install (Figure 1-7). To reduce installation size, I uncheck the "Android + Xamarin.Forms" entry and only install iOS- and macOS-related components. Then, after you click the *Install* button, the actual installation process begins.

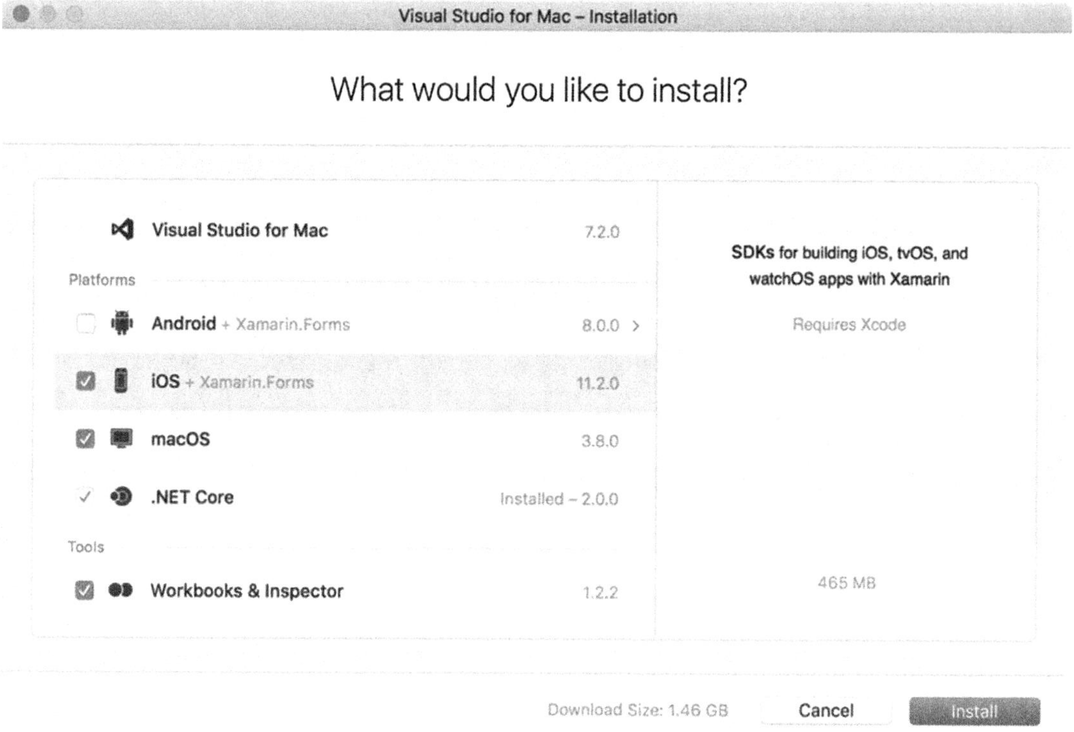

Figure 1-7. *Choosing components to install*

Visual Studio will now download and install the components. This will take a while, depending on network speed. You will be informed about each installation step and the overall progress, as shown in Figure 1-8. Also, as depicted in this figure, macOS may prompt you for the administrator password several times during installation. Once installation has finished, an appropriate dialog appears. Note that to build and run apps in the simulator, you will need to wait until Xcode installation has finished.

Figure 1-8. *Installing Visual Studio for Mac*

Hello, World! App

After installing the development tools, we can start building the first app. To jumpstart the Xamarin.iOS development, I will tell you how to create the project using the Single View app template. Then, we will supplement the app with a single button. This button will react to taps such that the native alert will be displayed. Subsequently, we will add specific actions to this alert. Displaying alerts is a typical functionality of not only introductory apps, but also real apps, where it is used to collect user input or get confirmation for performing irreversible operations.

Creating the Project

To create the project, open Visual Studio for Mac. A welcome screen, depicted in Figure 1-9, appears. Then, you either choose File/New Solution in the menu bar or click the *New Project* button, located under the "Recent" header. This activates the New Project window, shown in Figure 1-10.

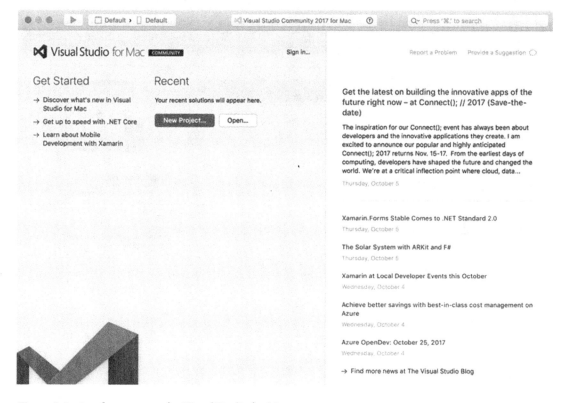

Figure 1-9. *A welcome screen for Visual Studio for Mac*

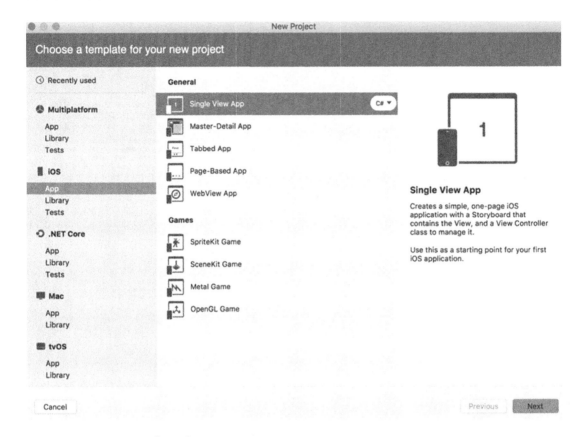

Figure 1-10. *Project template selection*

The New Project creator lets you choose a template for your project. To filter the list of templates to items directly related to iOS apps, you click *App entry* under the iOS tab. A list of available project templates will then appear on the right. This list is divided into two categories: General and Games. In this book, we will only use project templates from the General group. This category contains the following templates:

- Single View App — You use this template to create the app, which comprises a single view; i.e., an app without any navigation, like the app shown in Figure 1-1.

- Master-Detail App — This template creates apps that use Master-Detail interface. In such cases, a list displays short descriptions of objects. Once you choose an object from this list (master), corresponding details will be displayed in the dedicated area (detail). Master-Detail interface is used, for example, in the Stocks iOS app (Figure 1-11).

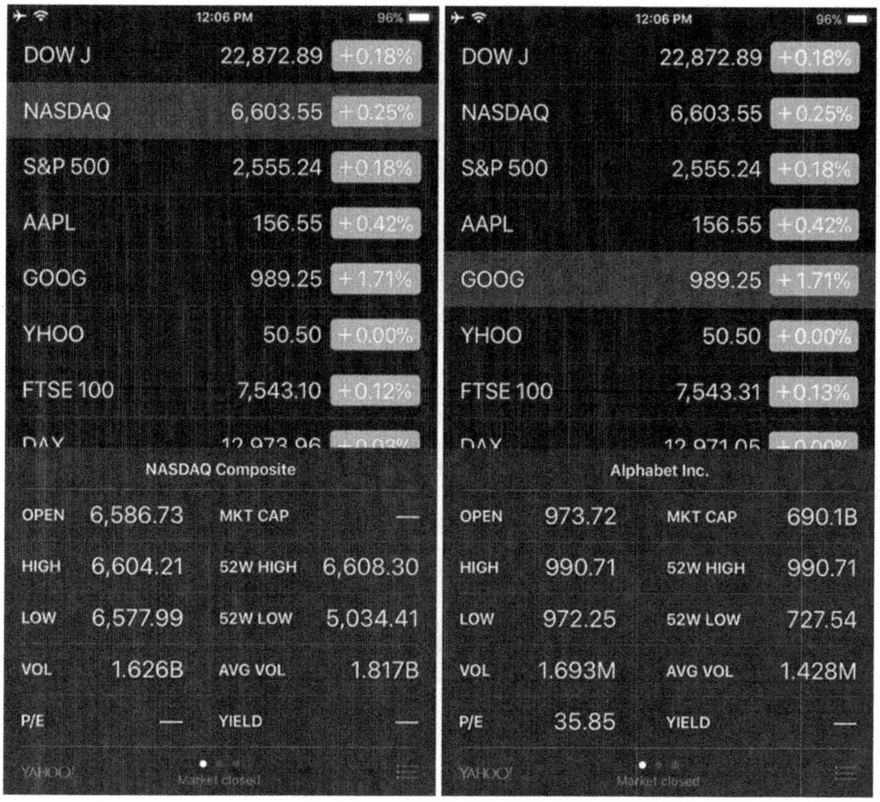

Figure 1-11. *Representational view of a Master-Detail iOS app. The list of objects (companies) is shown on top. When you tap any of these objects, corresponding details (stock values) appear at the bottom.*

- Tabbed App — You use this template to create a multi-tab application in which you can arrange visual controls in multiple tabs. User then navigates between tabs using labeled icons shown at the bottom of the screen. Such navigation is used in the Clock iOS app (Figure 1-12).

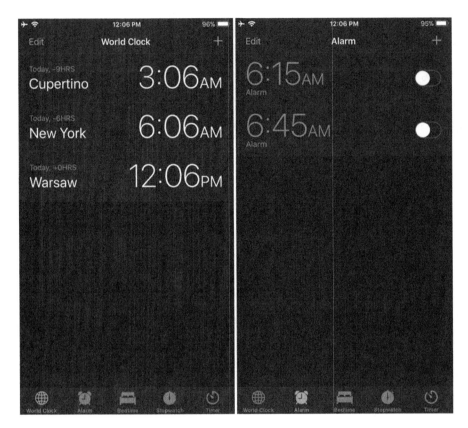

Figure 1-12. An example of Tabbed iOS application. You switch between tabs using labeled icons displayed in the bottom part of the view

- Page-based App — Use this template to create a multi-view app in which controls are arranged in pages. The user swipes between pages with touch gestures. For instance, such page-based navigation is utilized in the Weather iOS app, shown in Figure 1-13.

Figure 1-13. *Page-based navigation is utilized in the Weather app to switch between weather forecasts*

- WebView App — You use this template to jumpstart hybrid app development. This project template creates a view with an embedded WebView control. The latter renders a website written with HTML, CSS, and JavaScript. I will tell you more about WebView in Chapter 3.

To proceed further, let's pick the Single View app project template and keep the default language selection of C#. Then, you will have the option to specify the name of your app and organization identifier (Figure 1-14). I set these values to HelloWorld and com.db, respectively. The next group of controls in app configuration lets you specify which devices will be supported by your app. In this case, I made my app universal and chose iPad and iPhone. The very last control in the app configuration screen is the Target drop-down list. You use this list to select the minimum iOS version that will be supported by your app. I set this to iOS 9.0. After configuring the app, press the *Next* button, which activates the view depicted in Figure 1-15.

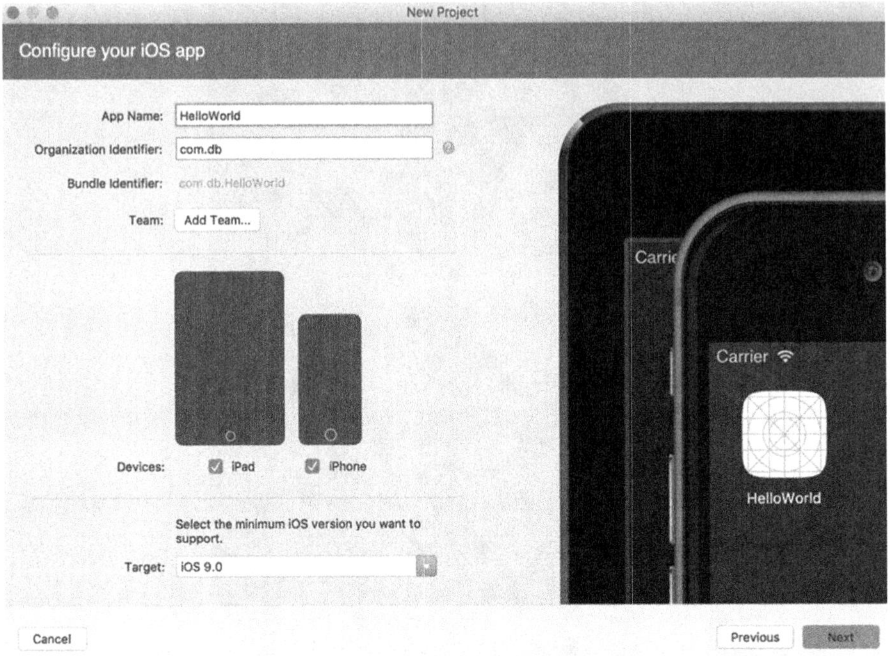

Figure 1-14. *iOS app configuration*

The Project Summary window shown in Figure 1-15 displays the project and solution names. You can also use this screen to set the location for your source code, enable version control, and add an automated UI test project. Here, I keep the settings at their default values. I will tell you more about unit testing in Chapter 6. So, go ahead and press the *Create* button to proceed further. You will quickly see the Getting Started screen of Visual Studio (Figure 1-16).

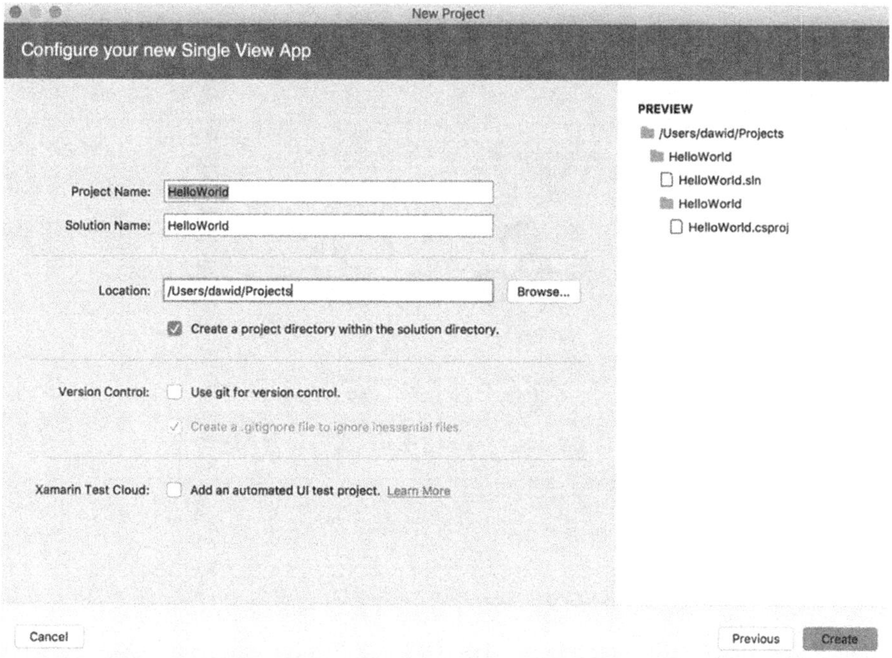

Figure 1-15. *Project summary*

The Getting Started screen displays several options for you. Specifically, it lets you start designing the user interface (UI) of your app, add a mobile backend, and unit test the project. Also, on the left-hand side of this window you will see the Solution Explorer, which displays the structure of the HelloWorld app. Specifically, there is a HelloWorld solution, under which you can find the project of the same name (refer to Figure 1-15). This project contains the files that make up your app. They are discussed in more detail in the next chapter. For now, let's create a simple UI for the HelloWorld app using the Storyboard (or iOS) Designer.

Figure 1-16. *HelloWorld project open in Visual Studio*

Storyboard Designer

To start creating the UI, you can click the *Open Storyboard Designer* button. This will open the `Main.storyboard` file and activate the Visual Interface or Storyboard Designer (or simply iOS Designer) of Visual Studio. This designer is shown in Figure 1-17. Three elements of this designer should be discussed in more detail, as follows:

- Visual preview of the app. This element covers the central part of the designer and lets you see how your views will be displayed in the device without your having to run your app. For multi-view apps, the visual preview will also depict the relationships between views (tabs or pages) through which the user can navigate.

- Toolbox, which is in the top-right corner, contains a list of visual objects you can drag on the view.

- Properties window, located below the Toolbox. You use the Properties window to change the appearance of and configure visual controls, to define the layout, and to wire methods to events (like tap or input) fired by controls.

Note that you can also activate the preceding windows or pads using an appropriate menu option in Visual Studio: View ➤ Pads (see Figure 1-18). There is also one useful drop-down list in the preview mode. That is the View As list, which you can find on the top pane of the visual preview. The View As drop-down list lets you choose the device type to use for the preview. As shown in Figure 1-17, I set this device to iPhone 6.

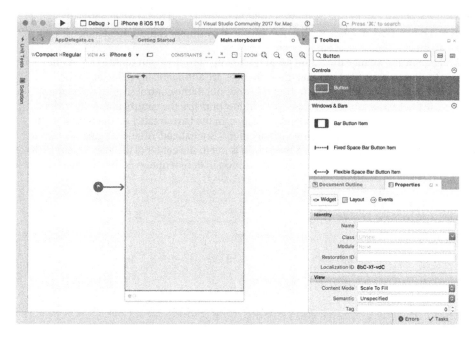

Figure 1-17. *Storyboard editor*

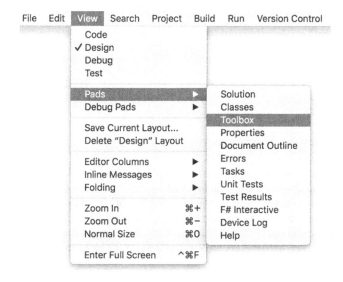

Figure 1-18. *View menu of Visual Studio*

User Interface

To proceed further, let's add the button to the view. You can do so by dragging the button control from the toolbox onto the view. You can then modify the visual appearance of the button using the Properties window after clicking the inserted control. As shown in Figure 1-19, the content of the Properties window is partitioned into three tabs: Widget, Layout, and Events. You use the first tab to adjust the identity and visual appearance. The Layout tab allows you to specify the control's dimensions and its arrangement with respect to other controls. The last tab, Events, displays the list of events fired by the specific control along with the methods associated with these events; i.e., event handlers.

First, go to the Widget tab and change the Name property (Identity group) to `ButtonAlert` and title property (Button group) to `Hello, World!` Note that these changes are automatically reflected in the preview window. Specifically, you will see that the button title does not fit the control size. To resize the visual control, you can use the Layout tab of the Properties window or resize the control manually in the preview window. I resized the button using the first option. Hence, in the Layout tab, I set the button width to 100, leaving other parameters (like X, Y, height, and arrangement) unchanged. After changing the button size, the internal text becomes fully visible. However, the button is not in the center of the view anymore. To put it back to the center you can press the first button in the Position in Parent option of the Arrange section (see right part of Figure 1-19).

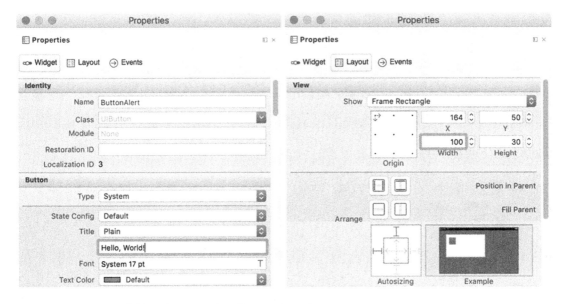

Figure 1-19. *Widget (left) and Layout tabs of button-control properties*

With the button adjusted we can create the first event handler, which will display the message to the user. You can do so in two ways. The easiest one is to double-click the button in preview mode. This will switch the view to display the contents of `ViewController.cs`. Additionally, a small popup window titled "Add event handler" appears. As shown in Figure 1-20, you can use the arrow keys to specify the location it should go in the source-code file, and Visual Studio will insert a definition of the default event handler. I placed this event handler below the previous method, `DidReceiveMemoryWarning`. So, my `ViewController.cs` looks as shown in Listing 1-1.

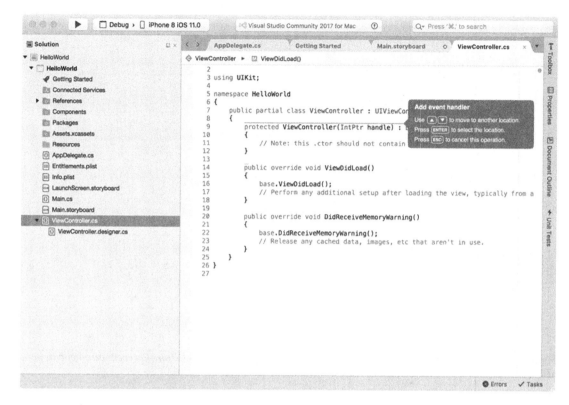

Figure 1-20. *Adding an event handler*

Listing 1-1. A Default ViewController Class Supplemented by TouchUpInside Event Handler

```
public partial class ViewController : UIViewController
{
    // Other methods are shown in Figure 1-20.

    partial void ButtonAlert_TouchUpInside(UIButton sender)
    {
        throw new NotImplementedException();
    }
}
```

As you see in Listing 1-1, this new event handler is associated with the TouchUpInside event (also see Figure 1-21).

The alternative way of adding an event handler is through the Events tab of the Properties window. You would only need to type the name of the event handler and press *Enter*. It is also important to note that, once you create an event handler, it can be associated with other events. To this end, use the drop-down list, which is populated by available event handlers (Figure 1-21).

When you double-click a control in preview mode, Visual Studio automatically creates the event handler, depending on the control type. This event handler is called "default event handler" because it is related to the common usage of a particular control. In the case of a button, the default event handler is "Up Inside." I will show you more examples of event handlers in Chapter 3.

Figure 1-21. *Events tab of button properties. Note that the ButtonAlert_TouchUpInside event handler can be also associated with Up Outside event.*

AlertViewController

We are now ready to replace the default definition of the ButtonAlert_TouchUpInside event handler we created in the previous subsection. The logic we implement will display a native alert window that will present the Hello, Xamarin.iOS! message. To display such an alert, you first create and configure an instance of the UIAlertViewController class and then show it to the user with the PresentViewController method. A complete example appears in Listing 1-2.

Listing 1-2. Creating and Displaying an Alert Window

```
private const string title = "Apress";
private const string message = "Hello, Xamarin.iOS!";

partial void ButtonAlert_TouchUpInside(UIButton sender)
{
    var alertController = UIAlertController.Create(
        title, message, UIAlertControllerStyle.Alert);

    PresentViewController(alertController, false, null);
}
```

To create an instance of the UIAlertController class I use its Create static method. This method accepts three arguments: title, message, and UIAlertControllerStyle. The purpose of the first two arguments is rather obvious. They specify the title and the message of the alert. The last argument, UIAlertControllerStyle, is the enumeration you use to define the alert style. You can choose between Alert or ActionSheet. Here, I set the alert style to UIAlertControllerStyle.Alert. In the next subsection,

I will create the action sheet, and, therefore, I saved title and message in corresponding fields of the ViewController class.

To display an alert, I use PresentViewController, which is implemented within the UIViewController class, the base class of the ViewController class associated with a default view of the HelloWorld app. As shown in Listing 1-2, the PresentViewController method accepts the following three arguments:

- viewControllerToPresent is the object, deriving from the UIViewController class, representing a view controller to be presented.

- animated indicates whether the view controller should be presented with animation or not.

- completionHandler is the action to be executed after animation is done.

You can now test the preceding solution in the device emulator. To run the app, click the *Play* button in the Debug toolbar (Figure 1-22). This toolbar is located inside the top pane of Visual Studio. You use the Target toolbar not only to run the app but also to set configuration (Debug or Release) and choose target device. Here, I set the target device to iPhone 8 with iOS 11.0, but you can choose any other simulator. For instance, to create screenshots from Figure 1-1 I used iPhone X simulator.

Figure 1-22. *A target toolbar*

When you press the *Play* button it changes to a *Stop* button, and the device simulator will be started. Subsequently, the HelloWorld app will be executed (Figure 1-23), so you can click the *Hello, World!* Button. As a result, the alert will be displayed (right part of Figure 1-23).

Figure 1-23. *HelloWorld app running in the iPhone simulator*

As you will quickly find out, the alert window blocks the app; there is not yet a button or control to close the alert. Thus, to break the app execution you need to either click the *Stop* button in the Debug toolbar or double press the SHIFT + COMMAND + H keyboard short key on your PC or double press a *Home* button on the simulator. The simulator screen takes the form depicted in Figure 1-24. You can then swipe up the HelloWorld app to kill its process.

At this point, it is also good to note that you can use the device simulator to emulate various user actions. For instance, you can emulate shake gesture, Touch ID, Apple Pay, or simply rotate or reboot a device. You can access these options through the Hardware menu of the simulator.

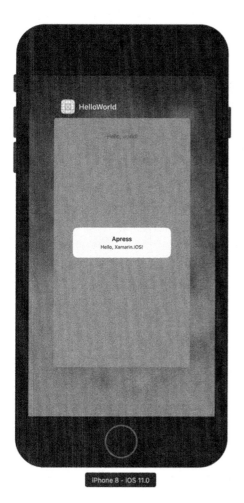

Figure 1-24. *Multi-tasking management in iPhone simulator*

Actions

Let's now add an action to the alert view. This action will enable the user to close the alert window instead of killing the whole app process. In practice, an action will appear as the button within the alert window. When you press this button, the alert window is closed and additional custom code can be executed. Exemplary usage of such an action is presented in Listing 1-3, which shows an extended implementation of the alert creation. Similarly, as before, I created the action outside the event handler to reuse an action later. If you now re-run the app in the simulator, the alert will be supplemented by the OK button (Figure 1-25).

Listing 1-3. Adding a Default Action to the Alert

```
private const string title = "Apress";
private const string message = "Hello, Xamarin.iOS!";
private UIAlertAction okAction =
    UIAlertAction.Create("OK", UIAlertActionStyle.Default, null);
```

```
partial void ButtonAlert_TouchUpInside(UIButton sender)
{
    var alertController = UIAlertController.Create(
        title, message, UIAlertControllerStyle.Alert);

    alertController.AddAction(okAction);

    PresentViewController(alertController, false, null);
}
```

Figure 1-25. *An alert with a default action*

As Listing 1-3 shows, to create an action you use the UIAlertAction class. In particular, this class implements the static Create method, which accepts three arguments, as follows:

- title — Use this argument to specify the action title; i.e., action's caption displayed in the alert.

- style — This defines action style or type. All available action types are represented as values of the UIAlertStyle enumeration. This enumeration defines typical actions, which are taken depending on the user input:

  - Cancel — This type indicates that a given operation should be canceled and that associated application state or data should be left unchanged.

  - Default — This is a default action for the particular alteration of the application state.

  - Destructive — This type is typically used to confirm deletion of specific application data.

- handler allows you to define a set of statements, which are invoked when the action button is tapped by the user.

In Listing 1-3, I created a single Default action with OK title, which does not invoke any further logic (handler argument is null). Of course, you can add more actions. We will use this possibility in the next subsection while creating the action sheet.

Action Sheet

Action sheet is another style for iOS alerts. According to Apple guidelines, an action sheet should be used to present a few choices for the user depending on the current context. In particular, you use such an object to get confirmation of deleting specific elements of the app data. You create the action sheet analogously as an alert, namely by using UIAlertController class. To explicitly show that, let's now supplement the HelloWorld app with another button, which, when tapped, will display an action sheet. To this end, go to the Storyboard Editor by double-clicking Main.storyboard in the Solution Explorer. Then, add the second button and place it below the ButtonAlert. Change the name and title of the new button to ButtonActionSheet and ActionSheet, respectively. Adjust its width and location and then create the default event handler (place it below ButtonAlert_TouchUpInside). Modify the definition of this handler as shown in Listing 1-4. Finally, you can rerun the app, and you will get the results previously depicted in Figure 1-1.

Listing 1-4. Creating the UIAlertViewController Using the Class Constructor

```
private UIAlertAction cancelAction =
    UIAlertAction.Create("Cancel", UIAlertActionStyle.Cancel, null);

partial void ButtonActionSheet_TouchUpInside(UIButton sender)
{
    var actionSheetController = new UIAlertController()
    {
        Title = title,
        Message = message
    };
```

```
actionSheetController.AddAction(okAction);
actionSheetController.AddAction(cancelAction);

PresentViewController(actionSheetController, true, null);
}
```

Listing 1-4 presents an alternative way of creating an instance of the UIAlertController class. I used the parameterless constructor of this class and then modified the Title and Message properties of the resulting object. Note that there is no property to configure the alert style, which in this case is set to UIAlertControllerStyle.ActionSheet by default. Of course, you can still use the Create method UIAlertController to create an action sheet, but you would need to replace the last parameter with UIAlertControllerStyle.ActionSheet (refer back to Listing 1-2).

In the preceding example, I supplemented the alert sheet by two actions: one created with a default style (okAction), and the other built with a cancel style (cancelAction). You can note a difference in the appearance of the buttons associated with these actions in Figure 1-1. The *Cancel* button is distinguished with respect to the *OK* button.

Finally, to present an action sheet, I use the same method as before, PresentViewController, but I changed its second argument to true so the alert presentation will be animated. After re-running the app, you will get the results shown previously in Figure 1-1.

Summary

In this chapter, we prepared a development environment, which will be utilized in the next chapters. We then discussed available project templates for creating iOS apps and implemented our first Single View HelloWorld app, which displays various alerts. In the next chapter, using the source code developed here we will analyze the app structure and discuss the most important elements of every Xamarin.iOS app.

CHAPTER 2

■ ■ ■

App Structure and Lifecycle

In this chapter, you will learn about the most important elements of an app and relationships between them. We will begin by exploring the app entry point and how Xamarin.iOS interfaces with the native iOS SDK. Subsequently, we will learn about the app and view lifecycles, declaration of app capabilities, and properties to reach the storyboards. Additionally, we will analyze the Model View Controller (MVC) design pattern utilized in programming for the Apple platforms. Lastly, we will combine the view lifecycle with the MVC pattern to store data in a device's memory.

An Entry Point

The HelloWorld app, similar to any other C# app, begins its execution from the static `Main` method of the `Application` class. This applies regardless of whether you are creating a console application, Universal Windows Platform app, ASP.NET web application, or .NET Core or Xamarin.iOS app. All of these apps utilize the `Application.Main` method as an entry point. However, the particular implementation of this method varies between those app types. In the case of Xamarin.iOS, the implementation of the `Main` method is tailored to the iOS platform. More specifically, as Listing 2-1 shows, the `Application.Main` method invokes the function of the same name from the `UIApplication` class. The `UIApplication` class encapsulates the main processing loop of the Xamarin.iOS app. This processing loop, as in all other apps with a graphical user interface, handles all the events related to the app lifecycle (activation, switching between foreground and background), events triggered by the user (like touch, inputting data, switching between views), or the operating system (OS restarts, memory warnings).

Importantly, every iOS app creates only one instance of the `UIApplication` class or its subclass. Internally, the `UIApplication` class uses another class, which implements the `UIApplicationDelegate` interface. The latter object is dedicated to handling the app lifecycle. Therefore, the `Main` method from Listing 2-1, apart from command-line arguments (`args`, which is the array of strings), accepts two other parameters: `principalClassName` and `delegateClassName`. The first one specifies the name of the class deriving from `UIApplication`. If you want to use a default `UIApplication` class, then you pass null for `principalClassName`. The second argument, `delegateClassName`, lets you specify the name of the class implementing `UIApplicationDelegate`. By default, `delegateClassName` is set to AppDelegate. You will learn about this class later in this chapter, as this is a part of the HelloWorld and any other Xamarin.iOS project.

Listing 2-1. An Entry Point of the Xamarin.iOS App

```
namespace HelloWorld
{
    public class Application

    {
        static void Main(string[] args)
        {
            UIApplication.Main(args, null, "AppDelegate");
        }
    }
}
```

To explain what an encapsulation of the processing loop means, let's analyze the source code of Xamarin.iOS, which is available here: `http://bit.ly/xamarin_ios_code`. This analysis also helps us to better understand what Xamarin.iOS really is. In particular, the definition of `UIApplicationClass` (`http://bit.ly/UiApplication`) shows that its `Main` method (Listing 2-2), after obtaining handles to the principal and delegate class names, invokes another version of the `Main` method. The latter, as depicted in Listing 2-3, first invokes the `Initialize` method. This method configures thread-synchronization context, which is used to update controls through the UI thread. Then, the `Main` method invokes the `UIApplicationMain` function, which is declared in an external, Objective-C library. This library comes from the iOS SDK. You now see that Xamarin.iOS, in the simplest definition, is the set of C# bindings to the native iOS SDK exposed through Objective-C libraries. Therefore, Xamarin.iOS lets you develop native apps with full access to the platform's SDK. For this reason, Xamarin apps are referred to as native mobile apps.

Listing 2-2. A Definition of the UIApplication.Main Method Invoked in the Entry Point of HelloWorld App

```
public static void Main(string[] args, string principalClassName,
    string delegateClassName)
{
    IntPtr principal = principalClassName != null ?
        new NSString(principalClassName).Handle : IntPtr.Zero;
    IntPtr delegatec = delegateClassName != null ?
        new NSString(delegateClassName).Handle : IntPtr.Zero;
    Main(args, principal, delegatec);
}
```

Listing 2-3. An Actual Call to the UIApplicationMain Method Implemented in the Objective-C Library from the iOS SDK

```
static void Main(string[] args, IntPtr principal, IntPtr @delegate)
{
    Initialize();
    UIApplicationMain(args.Length, args, principal, @delegate);
}

[DllImport("__Internal")]
extern static int UIApplicationMain(int argc, string[] argv,
    IntPtr principalClassName, IntPtr delegateClassName);
```

To invoke a function from the Objective-C library you use the Platform Invocation Services (P/Invoke). In this mechanism, you first declare the C# method with extern and static keywords and decorate this declaration with the DllImportAttribute. This attribute is used to specify the physical location of the library to load DllImportAttribute can be optionally used to specify a name of the function exported by this library in case this name differs from a method you declare in the C# code. Once you have this declaration, you call an external function by invoking the C# method, exactly the same as in Listing 2-3. However, as we see in Listing 2-3, the DllImportAttribute of the C# method does not include a path to the external library. Instead, it uses the __Internal string. This instructs P/Invoke to load a function from the static library, which compiles into an application.

But wait, how is my C# code turned into the actual iPhone or iPad application? This is done automatically when we compile the project in Visual Studio through the tool called *mtouch*. Mtouch is the command-line program that changes your C# .NET code into the app bundle, which is then executed by iOS. In the case of the HelloWorld app, we compiled for the simulator; the bundle can be found under the following subfolder of the HelloWorld project: bin\iPhoneSimulator\Debug\device-builds\ iphone9.1-10.3\HelloWorld.app. If you open this folder, you will see a number of files. For now, let's just point out the relevant ones. First, the app bundle contains Xamarin.iOS.dll, which has bindings to the iOS SDK. Second, there is an mscorlib.dll file. It implements the Microsoft Common Object Runtime Library, a runtime for all Microsoft .NET applications. Finally, there are several other .NET libraries, like System. dll, System.Core.dll, and System.Xml.dll. They are referenced in the HelloWorld app project to use basic types and functionality from the .NET framework.

Now that we have a solid understanding of the most important behind-the-scenes aspects of Xamarin. iOS, we can move forward to learn about the AppDelegate class.

AppDelegate

To discuss the AppDelegate class, let's open the AppDelegate.cs file from the HelloWorld project. First, when inspecting the class declaration, you will see that the AppDelegate implements the UIApplicationDelegate interface. Second, the AppDelegate declaration is decorated with the RegisterAttribute. It is implemented within the Xamarin.iOS and is used to register a class to the Objective-C runtime. This registration is required since an instance of the AppDelegate class is passed to the UIApplicationMain Objective-C function. Third, the AppDelegate implements a single property, Window, of type UIWindow. UIWindow represents the container for views found in the iOS apps. So, you use this property to control that container. Last, AppDelegate overrides a number of methods from the UIApplicationDelegate. You use these methods to handle particular application events during the app lifecycle. To explicitly show how these lifecycles proceed, let's modify AppDelegate according to Listing 2-4.

Listing 2-4. Modified Definition of the AppDelegate Class

```
using System.Diagnostics;
using Foundation;
using UIKit;

namespace HelloWorld
{
    [Register("AppDelegate")]
    public class AppDelegate : UIApplicationDelegate
    {
        public override UIWindow Window { get; set; }

        public override bool WillFinishLaunching(
            UIApplication application, NSDictionary launchOptions)
        {
```

```csharp
        DisplayInfo("WillFinishLaunching", application);

        return true;
    }

    public override bool FinishedLaunching(
        UIApplication application, NSDictionary launchOptions)
    {
        DisplayInfo("FinishedLaunching", application);

        return true;
    }

    public override void OnResignActivation(
        UIApplication application)
    {
        DisplayInfo("OnResignActivation", application);
    }

    public override void DidEnterBackground(
        UIApplication application)
    {
        DisplayInfo("DidEnterBackground", application);
    }

    public override void WillEnterForeground(
        UIApplication application)
    {
        DisplayInfo("WillEnterForeground", application);
    }

    public override void OnActivated(UIApplication application)
    {
        DisplayInfo("OnActivated", application);
    }

    public override void WillTerminate(UIApplication application)
    {
        DisplayInfo("WillTerminate", application);
    }

    private void DisplayInfo(string eventName,
        UIApplication application)
    {
        Debug.WriteLine($"App event: {eventName}."
            + $"App state: {application.ApplicationState}");
    }
    }
}
```

In Listing 2-4, there is one new public method, WillFinishLaunching, and one private method, DisplayInfo. WillFinishLaunching handles the corresponding app event, while DisplayInfo is implemented to present information about the application event. Therefore, this method is invoked within each application event handler, being an overriden version of appropriate event handler from the base class (UIApplicationDelegate). Note that I always pass the name of the application event to the first argument of DisplayInfo. This method then prints the event name along with the application state in the application output. To that end, I use the WriteLine method of the System.Diagnostics.Debug class. To obtain an application's state, I read the corresponding property of the UIApplication class. An instance of this class is passed to the second argument of the DisplayInfo method.

Application states are represented by the following values of the UIApplicationState enumeration:

- Active – The app is running in the foreground and responds to user actions. This means that the app UI is visible to the user, and the user can interact with the app.

- Inactive – The app is running in the foreground but does not respond to user actions. In such cases, the UI can be still visible, but the app does not respond. This can happen, for example, when you activate multitask selection in your phone or simulator (refer back to Figure 1-24).

- Background – The app is running in the background, so its UI is invisible. However, the app can perform some sort of background operation like fetching data from an external web service.

Let's now see at what point the application event handlers are invoked during the application lifecycle. To this end, let's start the app in a simulator and open Application Output. By default, this output is undocked and minimized, so to activate this window you will need to click Application Output ➤ HelloWorld bar, which is located in the bottom right part of the Visual Studio screen (Figure 2-1).

■ Application Output - HelloWorld

```
Loaded assembly: /Library/Frameworks/Xamarin.Interactive.framework/
Loaded assembly: /Library/Frameworks/Xamarin.Interactive.framework/
App event: WillFinishLaunching. App state: Inactive
App event: FinishedLaunching. App state: Inactive
App event: OnActivated. App state: Active
App event: OnResignActivation. App state: Active
App event: DidEnterBackground. App state: Background
App event: WillEnterForeground. App state: Background
App event: OnActivated. App state: Active
App event: OnResignActivation. App state: Active
App event: DidEnterBackground. App state: Background
App event: WillTerminate. App state: Background
```

Figure 2-1. *HelloWorld Application Output, showing the app lifecycle*

Right after running the app, you will see that there are three app events reported: WillFinishLaunching, FinishedLaunching, and OnActivated (Figure 2-1). The first, the WillFinishLaunching event handler, is invoked when the UIApplication gets created. Subsequently, after the app has launched, another method, FinishedLaunching, is invoked. Typically, this method is used to create the app window and display a view by setting the RootViewController property of the Window class. However, the HelloWorld app was created using a template. In such a case, the default view is configured in the main storyboard. As I will explain later, this is done by setting the initialViewController attribute of the document XML tag. Note that the app is inactive until it is activated. An app activation is reported by the dedicated event, OnActivated. Once the app is active, its UI becomes visible, and you can start tapping the buttons we created previously. The app will respond to your requests.

By comparing the definitions of WillFinishLaunching and FinishedLaunching to all other event handlers related to the app lifecycle, we can see that they contain an additional argument, launchOptions. This argument is of type NSDictionary and comprises a set of key–value entries. These entries allow you to determine how your app was launched and what kind of launch parameters were passed to the app. You can find a list of all available keys along with an example of how to use them here: http://bit.ly/launch_options.

Let's now see what happens when we send the app to the background. You can do this in the simulator by pressing the following keyboard shortcut keys: COMMAND + SHIFT + H. The app will disappear, and you will see that another two event handlers are invoked: OnResignActivation and DidEnterBackground. You use the first one to save the application state or release any resources that the app does not need when inactive. After OnResignActivation, the DidEnterBackground app event is raised. It informs you that the app state has been changed to background (refer back to Figure 2-1).

You can now send the HelloWorld app to the foreground by pressing its icon in the simulator (see Figure 2-2). Another two app events are fired: WillEnterForeground and OnActivated. They correspond to the two app events raised when the app was put in the background, so their usage is reversed. Namely, WillEnterForeground informs you that the app is about to enter the foreground so you can use the appropriate event handler to restore the app state and prepare all the resources your app needs in the foreground. Subsequently, the app is activated, and you are notified about that through the OnActivated event.

Figure 2-2. *Simulator home screen with HelloWorld app icon*

Finally, let's see what happens when you kill the app through multitasking (which you can activate, as in the previous chapter, by clicking the home button twice). In such a case, three events are reported: OnResignActivation, DidEnterBackground, and WillTerminate. The first two are raised when you activate multitasking. So, up to this point, everything works the same as it would if you just put your app in the background. Once the app is about to terminate, an additional event is raised, WillTerminate. You use this event to clean up any resources used when your app was working in the background.

View Lifecycle

In the previous section, we learned about the app lifecycle. A similar mechanism is also available for individual views. View events are represented by appropriate event handlers implemented in the UIViewController class. You override these handlers in the derived class associated with the particular view (its view controller). Event handlers of the view lifecycle are utilized to prepare the view. For instance, you first restore data from a device's memory and then use these data to update controls. So, the controls are ready to present data before the view is presented to the user.

To demonstrate when particular view events are fired, I modify the source code of the ViewController class by adding methods from Listing 2-5. Again, there is one private helper method, DisplayInfo. It is used to display the name of the actual view event. Then, I use this method in the following five view event handlers: ViewDidLoad, ViewWillAppear, ViewDidAppear, ViewWillDisappear, and ViewDidDisappear. Therefore, I can track the view lifecycle.

Listing 2-5. Handling the View Lifecycle

```
public override void ViewDidLoad()
{
    base.ViewDidLoad();

    DisplayInfo("ViewDidLoad");
}

public override void ViewWillAppear(bool animated)
{
    base.ViewWillAppear(animated);

    DisplayInfo("ViewWillAppear");
}

public override void ViewDidAppear(bool animated)
{
    base.ViewDidAppear(animated);

    DisplayInfo("ViewDidAppear");
}

public override void ViewWillDisappear(bool animated)
{
    base.ViewWillDisappear(animated);

    DisplayInfo("ViewWillDisappear");
}

public override void ViewDidDisappear(bool animated)
{
    base.ViewDidDisappear(animated);

    DisplayInfo("ViewDidDisappear");
}

private void DisplayInfo(string eventName)
{
    Debug.WriteLine($"View event: {eventName}");
}
```

Note that in order to use the `Debug` class you will need to import the `System.Diagnostics` namespace by supplementing the file header with the following statement:

```
using System.Diagnostics;
```

After re-running the app in the simulator, we will see a list of app and view events in the Application Output Window (Figure 2-3). As we can expect, the first view event handler, `ViewDidLoad`, is invoked right after the app is loaded. Then, when the view is loaded, another two events are fired: `ViewWillAppear` and `ViewDidAppear`. You use them to implement a logic that prepares the view before it is displayed to the user.

To induce other view events, `ViewWillDisappear` and `ViewDidDisappear`, I terminated the app using iOS multitasking. So, `ViewWillDisappear` and `ViewDidDisappear` events are invoked right after the app enters the background (see bottom lines of the application output in Figure 2-3).

▪ Application Output - HelloWorld

```
App event: WillFinishLaunching. App state: Inactive
App event: FinishedLaunching. App state: Inactive
View event: ViewDidLoad
View event: ViewWillAppear
App event: OnActivated. App state: Active|
View event: ViewDidAppear
App event: OnResignActivation. App state: Active
App event: DidEnterBackground. App state: Background
View event: ViewWillDisappear
View event: ViewDidDisappear
App event: WillTerminate. App state: Background
```

Figure 2-3. *Application output showing events fired during consecutive steps of the app and view lifecycles*

As I will show later in this chapter, `ViewWillDisappear` and `ViewDidDisappear` are employed to store data when or after the view disappears.

Information Property List

So far, we have only discussed files that contained the C# code. However, the HelloWorld project also has several other files, which are required by all iOS apps. One such file is the Information Property List (`Info.plist`). This file defines application configuration. When you double-click this file in the Solution Explorer, you will see the editor featured in Figure 2-4. This editor has the following tabs, which you use to configure different options:

- Application – You use this tab to specify the following:

  - App identity: application name, bundle identifier, and version

  - Deployment information: target iOS version, device family (iPhone, iPad, or Universal), the name of the storyboard, which defines the user interface of the app (main interface), available app orientations, and configure status bar appearance

  - App icons and launch images: used to specify the name of the collection with icons and the name of the storyboard, which will be displayed during app launch—the so-called launch or splash screen

- Artwork for iTunes

- Enable Game Center and Maps Integration and configure Background Modes.

- Advanced – In this tab you will configure the Document Types and Universal Type Identifiers (UTIs) of the files that your app will support. Document Types, like PDFs, are used to define files that your app will support. On the other hand, UTIs refer to custom file types. You can also use the Advanced tab to define URL schemas for your app.

- Source – This is the tab that you use to define custom properties for your app. This feature is required in order to access specific functionalities of the iOS, like geolocation of the device.

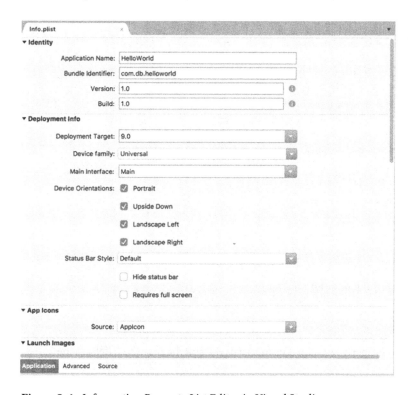

Figure 2-4. *Information Property List Editor in Visual Studio*

Entitlements Property List

Entitlements Property List, defined in the `Entitlements.plist` file, specifies the app's capabilities. When you open this file, Visual Studio for Mac activates the editor featured by Figure 2-5. This editor has two tabs: Application and Source. The first one is a graphical representation of various app capabilities (like iCloud integration or push notifications) you can enable, while the Source tab lets you define custom capabilities.

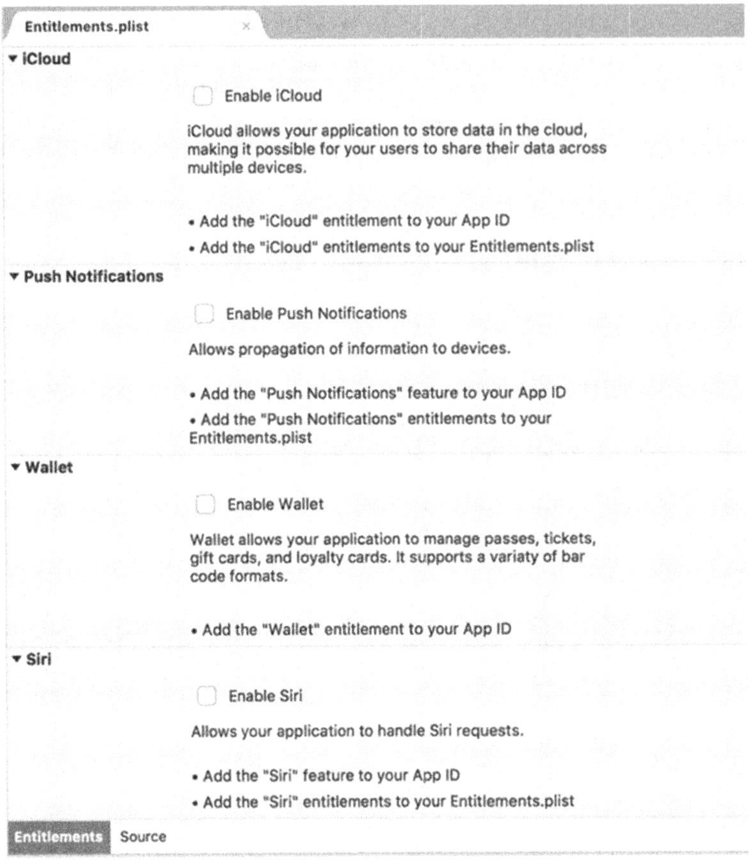

Figure 2-5. *Entitlements Property List Editor in Visual Studio*

Launch Storyboard

We have just seen that Information Property List allows us to specify the storyboard, which defines the launch screen. In the HelloWorld app, this storyboard is saved in LaunchScreen.storyboard. If you double-click this file in the Solution Explorer, the Visual Editor will open. This editor looks exactly the same as in the case of Main.storyboard, so you can define the Launch Screen in a similar manner. Let's use this opportunity to add the Image View, which will display an image when the app is being loaded. To add the Image View, you first locate this object in the Toolbox and then drag it onto the rectangle, representing the device. Subsequently, you can rescale it, so it fills the whole view, and then define the image to display. To select this image, you use the Image property of the Image View (Figure 2-6). By default, this entry is empty, and when you click it a file browser appears. Use this browser to pick any image you want. If this file is outside the target directory, the Add New File dialog, shown in Figure 2-7, will appear. iOS requires that all resources—the static files your app loads during runtime (like images)—should be stored under the Resources folder. Therefore, in the Add New File dialog, you need to choose the Copy option. An image file you selected will be then copied to the Resources subfolder of the HelloWorld app. Subsequently, the name of this file will appear in the drop-down list of the Image property (Figure 2-6).

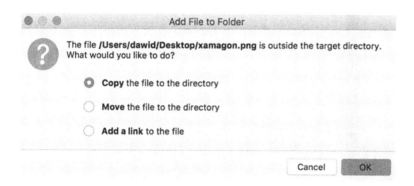

Figure 2-6. *Selected properties of the Image View*

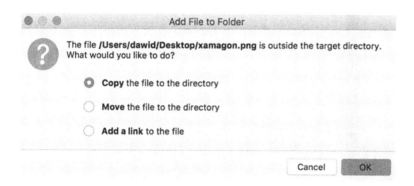

Figure 2-7. *Adding a resource file*

The Image View has a very important property, Content Mode (refer back to Figure 2-6). It controls how the image will be rescaled to fit the bounds of the Image View. Content Mode can take one of the following values defined in UIKit.UIViewContentMode:

- ScaleToFill – The image aspect ratio (a quotient of image width and height) will be adjusted to fill the whole area of the Image View.

- ScaleAspectFit – The image will be rescaled to fit the Image View, but the image aspect ratio will be preserved.

- ScaleAspectFill – The image will be rescaled and eventually cropped to fit the Image View.

- Redraw – The Image View will be redisplayed when its size changes.

- Center, Top, Bottom, Left, Right, TopLeft, TopRight, BottomLeft, BottomRight – These options define how the image will be aligned within the Image View.

37

In this example, I set the Content Mode to ScaleAspectFit. This is seen as the Aspect Fit option in Figure 2-7. In such a case, the aspect ratio of my image will not be changed, and therefore the image is located in the center of the screen, when the app is launching (Figure 2-8).

Figure 2-8. *Launch screen of the HelloWorld application*

Storyboards Under the Hood

A storyboard represents the whole user interface of an iOS app. In iOS, this user interface is composed of objects called *scenes*. A scene is the combination of a view controller and its associated views. The view controller displays and manages its views. In general, a storyboard can have multiple scenes (multiple view controllers and associated views). Transitions between these scenes are defined as *segues*.

We already used storyboards to define simple views, and we used the view controller to handle events (like tapping buttons) and view lifecycle management. A view controller plays one of the most important role in the iOS app, and therefore I used these two paragraphs to distinguish it from views, scenes, and segues.

You may actually wonder how it is possible to visually define a storyboard from Visual Studio. It is possible because the storyboard is written in XML format. Such an approach makes the storyboard portable and platform-independent. So, a storyboard can be edited manually or visually using a variety of tools.

Listing 2-6. Document Tag of Main.storyboard

```
<document type="com.apple.InterfaceBuilder3.CocoaTouch.Storyboard.XIB"
    version="3.0"
    toolsVersion="12120"
    systemVersion="16F73"
    targetRuntime="iOS.CocoaTouch"
    propertyAccessControl="none"
    useAutolayout="YES"
    useTraitCollections="YES"
    colorMatched="YES"
    initialViewController="BYZ-38-t0r">
```

To see the actual XML definition of the storyboard, right-click the storyboard file (Main.storyboard) in the Solution Explorer and then choose Open With/Source Code Editor from the context menu. The source code of the storyboard will be displayed. By inspecting the contents of this file, we can easily note that it has the typical hierarchical form of the XML file. There is one root node, xml, and right after it you can find the document tag, the declaration of which looks like the one from Listing 2-6. We see that this tag has a number of attributes, which, in particular, specify the document type, its version, target runtime, and identifier of the initial view controller. In the HelloWorld app we have a single view controller, so we actually did not to have to think about that. However, if an app has multiple view controllers, you can choose the initial one in the Visual Editor. You go there and then open the Properties window of the view controller. Subsequently, as Figure 2-9 shows, you check the "Is Initial View Controller" checkbox. The value of the initialViewController attribute will be updated automatically. That's why the HelloWorld app loads the ViewController as the first one. Consequently, its default view is presented after the app is launched.

Figure 2-9. *Properties of the View Controller. Note that "Is Initial View Controller" is checked, so a selected view associated with this view controller will appear as the first.*

Right after the document tag, we can see another tag, scenes. It contains a collection of scene objects, each of which is represented by the scene tag, whose sceneID attribute identifies the particular scene. Then, under the scene object, we can easily identify the viewController tag. It contains a child item and views, which contain a declaration of views associated with the view controller. In the HelloWorld app, the view controller has only one view, which hosts declarations of the two buttons we created. As Listing 2-7 shows, these declarations are within the subviews collection. Note that buttons are declared with a XML tag of the same name. This tag has a number of attributes that specify button parameters. Button size and location are then controlled by the child tag, rect. Title and color of the button caption are controlled by the state tag. There is also one other important tag, connections. It hosts actions (or events) associated with the particular button or another control. For each button, we have just a single action, which responds to the TouchUpInside event. Note that this action is further associated with the particular button or control through the connections collection defined right above the closing tag of viewController (Listing 2-8). Importantly, each element in this collection is represented by an outlet. This outlet, in the iOS nomenclature, wires an event fired by the control with its event handler. This connection was done automatically when we choose the event handler from the appropriate list of events in Visual Studio. Note that the destination attribute of each outlet precisely corresponds to the ID attributes of the button tag (Listing 2-7).

Listing 2-7. Subviews Collection

```
<subviews>
    <button contentMode="scaleToFill"
            contentHorizontalAlignment="center"
            contentVerticalAlignment="center"
            buttonType="roundedRect"
            lineBreakMode="middleTruncation"
            id="3"
            translatesAutoresizingMaskIntoConstraints="NO"
            fixedFrame="YES"
            opaque="NO">
        <rect key="frame" x="138" y="50"
                width="100" height="30"/>
        <autoresizingMask key="autoresizingMask"
                                    flexibleMaxX="YES"
                                    flexibleMaxY="YES"/>
        <state key="normal" title="Hello, World!">
            <color key="titleShadowColor"
                    white="0.5" alpha="1"
                    colorSpace="calibratedWhite"/>
        </state>
        <connections>
            <action selector="ButtonAlert_TouchUpInside:"
                    destination="BYZ-38-t0r"
                    id="6"
                    eventType="touchUpInside"/>
        </connections>
    </button>
    <!--Definition of ButtonActionSheet-->
</subviews>
```

Listing 2-8. A Collection of Outlets, Which Wire Control Events with Actions

```
<connections>
    <outlet property="ButtonAlert" destination="3" id="name-outlet-3"/>
    <outlet property="ButtonActionSheet" destination="10" id="name-outlet-10"/>
</connections>
```

The last interesting tag of the storyboard XML declaration is the `resources` collection. As Listing 2-9 shows, this collection contains a single entry that represents the image we used in the launch storyboard.

Listing 2-9. Resources Collection

```
<resources>
    <image name="xamagon.png" width="609" height="609"/>
</resources>
```

Model View Controller

So far, we have discussed the elements of the HelloWorld app that either constitute the app entry point or are related to views or view control. However, iOS apps very often cooperate with data. Apps need to retrieve data from internal or external storage or services and then display it to the user. The user can then modify this data, and the app has to reflect these changes in the storage it is cooperating with. This is a very common scheme for modern mobile apps, which constitute the end point of some larger system. Therefore, to simplify the app organization and improve its maintenance, iOS apps are built with the use of the Model View Controller (MVC) programming paradigm or design pattern. MVC divides the app into three main elements: View, Controller, and Model. General relationships between these elements as well as the data and signals flow are depicted in Figure 2-10. The controller is placed in the center because it plays the most important role. It displays views and handles user actions. These actions are mapped to event handlers and used to update the model, which represents the app state or some data set. A model notifies the controller whenever data was successfully updated or changed by some external process (another app or service). Controller uses these notifications to update its views.

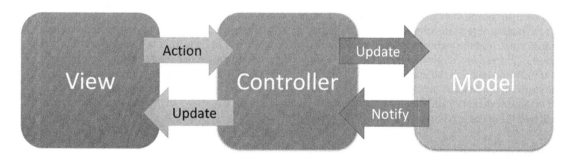

Figure 2-10. A general scheme of the Model View Controller programming paradigm

The MVC design pattern improves app maintenance thanks to the explicit separation of each layer. Consequently, each app layer can be developed and tested independently. This further helps you to reuse your code and better control your development.

Persisting Data

In this final subsection, I will tell you how to supplement the HelloWorld app with the simple model, Person. This class will contain two properties, which will store the person's first and last name. Then, in the default view, I will create two text-input fields, which will display a person's data and will let the user arbitrarily change them (Figure 2-11). The data will be stored in a file in the device's memory so that it can be restored after the app is restarted. The person's data will be stored and restored within the ViewWillDisappear and ViewWillAppear events of the view lifecycle.

Figure 2-11. *A HelloWorld app supplemented by additional controls for editing a person's data*

To implement the preceding solution, I first add the Person.cs file to the HelloWorld app. You can do this by clicking File ➤ New File from the Visual Studio menu. The dialog shown in Figure 2-12 appears. In this dialog, you pick the Empty Class item from the General tab and then change the class name to Person. After ensuring that the "Add to project" checkbox is selected, you click the *New* button.

Then, I implement the Person class (see companion code: Chapter_02/HelloWorld/Person.cs). As Listing 2-10 shows, this class derives from the NSCoding class. NSCoding provides a functionality for encoding and decoding objects in order to archive (store in file) or distribute them. Encoding means that the object is transformed into the architecture-independent byte stream, which can be further archived or transmitted to another process or a remote device. Then, the archived or received data is decoded such that the byte stream is transformed back to the particular object. In this case, the Person class has two public properties that will be stored in the device's memory: FirstName and LastName. For each property, I defined a key (saved in firstNameArchiveKey and lastNameArchiveKey), which identifies a property in the archive. This archive will be a file in the app temporary folder (archiveLocation field).

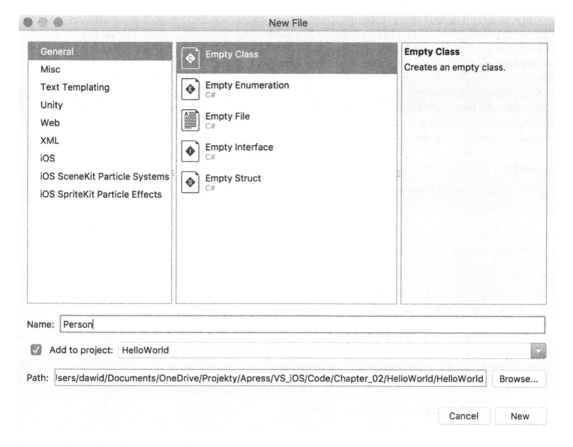

Figure 2-12. *A New File dialog of Visual Studio*

Listing 2-10. Declaration and Selected Elements of the Person Class

```
public class Person : NSCoding
{
    public string FirstName { get; set; } = string.Empty;
    public string LastName { get; set; } = string.Empty;

    private const string firstNameArchiveKey = "FirstName";
    private const string lastNameArchiveKey = "LastName";

    private string archiveLocation = Path.Combine(
        Path.GetTempPath(), "person");

    public Person() { }

    // Further definition of the Person class
}
```

To encode and decode string properties, I defined two methods in the Person class. Definitions of both methods appear in Listing 2-11. Let's see how the first method, EncodeString, works. This method invokes an Encode method of the Foundation.NSCoder class. NSCoder.Encode has several overloaded methods, which encode variables of several simple types. However, none of them can encode strings. Therefore, I had to convert a string to a byte array using the System.Text.Encoding class. Specifically, I use the GetBytes method of the UTF8 encoding. Then, I pass the result of this method to NSCoder.Encode along with the key used to identify the encoded value. The DecodeString method works in a reverse order. First, it uses a coder to retrieve the byte stream of the previously encoded value. Second, this byte stream is converted to a string with the UTF8.GetString method.

Listing 2-11. Encoding and Decoding String Properties

```
private void EncodeString(NSCoder encoder,
    string property, string propertyKey)
{
    var buffer = Encoding.UTF8.GetBytes(property);
    encoder.Encode(buffer, propertyKey);
}

private string DecodeString(NSCoder coder,
    string propertyKey)
{
    var result = string.Empty;

    var bytes = coder.DecodeBytes(propertyKey);
    if(bytes != null)
    {
        result = Encoding.UTF8.GetString(bytes);
    }

    return result;
}
```

The preceding methods are then utilized as shown in Listing 2-12. Namely, the DecodeString method is invoked within the Person class constructor. This constructor is exported as the initWithCoder Objective C initializer. This initializer is invoked automatically by the iOS runtime whenever you unarchive the object. A similar approach is used to encode an object. In such a case, you override the EncodeTo method, which comes from the NCoding class. This method is invoked when you archive the object. Therefore, in Listing 2-12 I use the EncodeString method to encode first and last name.

Listing 2-12. Decoding and Encoding a Person object

```
[Export("initWithCoder:")]
public Person(NSCoder coder)
{
    FirstName = DecodeString(coder, firstNameArchiveKey);
    LastName = DecodeString(coder, lastNameArchiveKey);
}
```

```
public override void EncodeTo(NSCoder encoder)
{
    EncodeString(encoder, FirstName, firstNameArchiveKey);
    EncodeString(encoder, LastName, lastNameArchiveKey);
}
```

To actually archive and unarchive an object, you use NSKeyedArchiver and NSKeyedUnarchiver, respectively. As Listing 2-13 shows, to archive an object in a file you use the ArchiveRootObjectToFile method of the NSKeyedArchiver class instance. Then, the object can be unarchived from the file with the UnarchiveFile method of the NSKeyedUnarchiver.

Listing 2-13. Archiving and Unarchiving a Person Object

```
public void StoreValues()
{
    NSKeyedArchiver.ArchiveRootObjectToFile(
        this, archiveLocation);
}

public void RestoreValues()
{
    if (NSKeyedUnarchiver.UnarchiveFile(archiveLocation)
        is Person retrievedPersonData)
    {
        FirstName = retrievedPersonData.FirstName;
        LastName = retrievedPersonData.LastName;
    }
}
```

After implementing the Person class, I supplement a default view of the HelloWorld app with two text fields and two labels. To that end, I use a storyboard visual designer in which I drag and drop two TextField and two Label objects onto the view. Then, I rename the text fields to TextFieldFirstName and TextFieldLastName, respectively. Last, I change the captions of the labels to *First name:* and *Last name:* and position the controls as shown in Figure 2-11.

As the next step, I modify the ViewController class as follows. First, I instantiate a Person class with a default parameterless constructor, and then I implement two helper methods: DisplayPersonData and StorePersonData. These methods are depicted in Listing 2-14. DisplayPersonData retrieves a person object from the file and then displays its name in the view by rewriting properties of the Person class instance as Text properties of the TextField controls. StorePersonData works in the opposite order—it rewrites data from text fields as properties of the Person class and then stores them in the file.

Listing 2-14. Storing and Restoring Person Data

```
private Person person = new Person();

private void DisplayPersonData()
{
    person.RestoreValues();

    TextFieldFirstName.Text = person.FirstName;
    TextFieldLastName.Text = person.LastName;
}
```

```
private void StorePersonData()
{
    person.FirstName = TextFieldFirstName.Text;
    person.LastName = TextFieldLastName.Text;

    person.StoreValues();
}
```

Finally, I need to invoke DisplayPersonData and StorePersonData, when the view appears and disappears, respectively. To that end, I employ corresponding view event handlers (Listing 2-15).

Listing 2-15. Utilizing View Lifecycle to Display and Store Person Data

```
public override void ViewWillAppear(bool animated)
{
    base.ViewWillAppear(animated);

    DisplayInfo("ViewWillAppear");

    DisplayPersonData();
}

public override void ViewWillDisappear(bool animated)
{
    base.ViewWillDisappear(animated);

    DisplayInfo("ViewWillDisappear");

    StorePersonData();
}
```

Now, when you run the app you can type any values into the two text fields. After closing the app and re-running it, you will see that these values are restored and displayed again in the UI.

Summary

In this chapter, you learned about app structure and lifecycle. You became more knowledgeable about the app entry point, the role of the AppDelegate class, and how you can define app properties and capabilities. We learned about the launch storyboard, and I described the internal structure of the main storyboard. Finally, we delved into the Model View Controller design pattern and used it, along with the view lifecycle, to persist data in a device's memory.

CHAPTER 3

■ ■ ■

Views

Fueled by knowledge about the iOS app structure, available project templates, and the app lifecycle, we can move forward to learn about creating complex views. We will start by learning how to use several basic controls, like switch or slider, and then investigate advanced controls, like table views, web views, and map views. Specifically, we will learn how to use tables to display collections of data. Web view will be utilized to render interactive web pages (Google Maps) in Xamarin.iOS apps. Lastly, we will use the map view to present a native iOS map. In this chapter, we will also learn how to define adaptive views, which automatically adjust to screens of various sizes and also to device orientation.

The name of almost every iOS control ends with "view"; for instance, Table View or Map View. Therefore, to save space I will quite often refer to them as table or map instead of using the fully qualified name.

Basic Controls

We have already worked with several basic controls, like buttons, labels, text fields, and images. In this section, I will show you another three controls: a switch, a slider, and a view. More specifically, I will tell you how to utilize these controls to create an app, shown in Figure 3-1. In this app, the orange view of square shape is translated when you change a slider value. The translation direction depends on the switch state—the square translates vertically if the switch is on, and horizontally otherwise. So, additionally, you will learn how to dynamically change the position of any control.

© Dawid Borycki 2018

D. Borycki, *Beginning Xamarin Development for the Mac*, https://doi.org/10.1007/978-1-4842-3132-6_3

Figure 3-1. *UI of the app illustrating sample usage of switch and slider*

To implement the app shown in Figure 3-1, I started by creating a new single view application (universal app compatible with iOS 9.0 and above) and set its name to InputControls. Then, I supplemented the main view of the app with four controls: switch, label, slider, and view (you can find all these controls in the toolbox). Controls were arranged as shown in Figure 3-1, and their properties were configured as follows:

- Switch:
  - Name: SwitchIsVertical
- Slider:
  - Name: SliderShift
- View:
  - Name: ViewMoveableSquare
  - Background: Orange
  - Width and height (Layout tab): 50

Given the UI, I start implementing the logic layer. To that end, I modify the definition of the ViewController class (ViewController.cs). I declare a private member initialSquareCenter and implement four helper methods (Listing 3-1 and Listing 3-2). Two methods from Listing 3-1 are used to store the initial location of the square and recenter it when user changes the translation direction with a switch. To obtain and update the location of the square, I use the Center property of the View control. This property is of type CoreGraphics.CGPoint, which is a struct representing a point in a plane. To use this type, you need to import the CoreGraphics namespace in the header of the ViewController.cs file:

```
using CoreGraphics;
```

Listing 3-1. Managing Initial Location of the Moveable Square (Orange View)

```
private CGPoint initialSquareCenter;

private void StoreSquareCenter()
{
    initialSquareCenter = ViewMoveableSquare.Center;
}

private void RecenterSquare()
{
    ViewMoveableSquare.Center = initialSquareCenter;
}
```

Two other helpers, shown in Listing 3-2, are utilized to actually translate the square over the available range. This range depends on the width (horizontal translation) or height (vertical translation) of the device's screen (see AdjustSliderRange method from Listing 3-2). I additionally reduce this range by a half of the square's side length, so the square will be always visible within the main view. To translate the square, I add the shift value (obtained from the slider value) to the X or Y coordinate of the initial square location. Effectively, this changes the point coordinates, and hence translates the square in a selected direction. As Listing 3-2 shows, I add the shift value to either the X or the Y property of the CGPoint (instantiated with initialSquareCenter), depending on the state of the switch control. If it is on (On property is true), I change the Y coordinate. Otherwise, I update the X coordinate.

Listing 3-2. Adjusting a Slider Range

```
private void AdjustSliderRange()
{
    var margin = ViewMoveableSquare.Frame.Width / 2.0;
    var range = SwitchIsVertical.On ? View.Frame.Height : View.Frame.Width;
    var maxShiftValue = Convert.ToInt32(range / 2.0 - margin);

    SliderShift.MinValue = -maxShiftValue;
    SliderShift.MaxValue = maxShiftValue;
    SliderShift.Value = 0;
}

private void TranslateSquare()
{
    var newCenter = new CGPoint(initialSquareCenter);

    if (!SwitchIsVertical.On)
    {
        newCenter.X += SliderShift.Value;
    }
    else
    {
        newCenter.Y += SliderShift.Value;
    }

    ViewMoveableSquare.Center = newCenter;
}
```

49

I use the preceding helper methods in the ViewDidLoad view event handler (Listing 3-3) and in two event handlers associated with the ValueChanged events of the switch and slider (Listing 3-4). I created these event handlers with the Events tab of the Control Properties pad. A default definition of ViewDidLoad was modified such that the initial position of the square is stored whenever the view is loaded. This is used to recenter the square within the view whenever the user taps a switch control. When the user changes a slider value, the second event handler from Listing 3-4 is invoked. This event handler uses the TranslateSquare method shown previously in Listing 3-2. So, when you run the app you will see the results shown in Figure 3-1.

Listing 3-3. Store Actual Square Position and Adjust Slider Range

```
public override void ViewDidLoad()
{
    base.ViewDidLoad();

    StoreSquareCenter();

    AdjustSliderRange();
}
```

Listing 3-4. Square Position Is Controled with Two Controls: Switch and Slider

```
partial void SwitchIsVertical_ValueChanged(UISwitch sender)
{
    RecenterSquare();

    AdjustSliderRange();
}

partial void SliderShift_ValueChanged(UISlider sender)
{
    TranslateSquare();
}
```

Tables

Many mobile apps are dedicated to displaying data obtained from web services. To display such data in an organized way, you typically use the Table View. In this section, I will tell you how to create a table presenting a list of colors along with their names (Figure 3-2). We will then modify the table's data source such that a user can delete and mark selected items and also obtain detailed information about the color through the UIAlertController. By completing this sample, you will know how to create tables that will respond to user requests via native iOS interfaces.

Figure 3-2. A list of predefined iOS colors displayed in a Table View

Displaying Items

To show how to use tables, I create a new single view iOS project and set its name to ColorsTable. Then, I add a new folder, Colors, in which I create three files: Color.cs, ColorsHelper.cs, and ColorsTableSource.cs. Each of these will store a definition of the appropriate class. I start by implementing the Color class, which is a helper object used to represent items in the table. As Listing 3-5 shows, the Color class has two public properties: Name and Value. Name stores a description of the color, while Value stores the actual color, represented as an instance of the UIColor class. UIColor, defined in the UIKit namespace, has a number of public static properties with predefined iOS colors. To get this list, I implement a ColorsHelper class (ColorsHelper.cs file), seen in Listing 3-6.

Listing 3-5. A Definition of the Color Class

```
using UIKit;

namespace ColorsTable.Colors
{
    public class Color
    {
        public string Name { get; set; }
        public UIColor Value { get; set; }
    }
}
```

The ColorsHelper class has only one public static method: GetColors. This method uses a C# reflection mechanism to read any information about all the public, static properties of the UIColor class. This information is represented as a collection of PropertyInfo objects. Each object of this type is then used to obtain the property name by simply reading the Name member and property value by invoking the GetValue method of the PropertyInfo class instance. These values are then utilized to create an instance of the Color class and add it to the resulting collection.

Listing 3-6. A List of Predefined iOS Colors Obtained with the C# Reflection Mechanism

```
using System.Collections.Generic;
using System.Reflection;
using UIKit;

namespace ColorsTable.Colors
{
    public static class ColorsHelper
    {
        public static List<Color> GetColors()
        {
            var colors = new List<Color>();

            var uiColorType = typeof(UIColor);

            var availableColors = uiColorType.GetProperties(
                BindingFlags.Public | BindingFlags.Static);

            foreach (var color in availableColors)
            {
                colors.Add(new Color()
                {
                    Name = color.Name,
                    Value = color.GetValue(uiColorType) as UIColor
                });
            }

            return colors;
        }
    }
}
```

Given the list of colors, I can now implement the collection of items for the Table View. To that end, I create the ColorsTableSource class, as shown in Listing 3-7. ColorsTableSource derives from the UITableViewSource and, because of that, has to implement two methods: RowsInSection and GetCell. The first one is used by the runtime to determine the number of rows in the current section of the table. The second one is invoked whenever the runtime is about to draw a cell for a particular row. Hence, in Listing 3-7, I use this method to prepare a cell using UITableViewCell. This class represents the visual appearance of the cell in a table. There are a few predefined cell styles you can use. They are represented by the following values from the UITableViewCellStyle enumeration (see Figure 3-3):

- **Default** – specifies that a cell contains a single, left-aligned text label and an optional image view

- **Value1** – specifies that a cell contains two labels: one that is left-aligned and the other that is right-aligned. The first label displays text you specify by setting the **Text** property of the **TextLabel** member of the **UITableView** class instance. To configure a string displayed by the second label, you use an **Text** property of the **DetailTextLabel**.

- **Value2** – uses a similar layout as **Value1,** but the first label is right-aligned while the second is left-aligned

- **Subtitle** – in this case, the **DetailTextLabel** is right below **TextLabel**, and both labels are left-aligned.

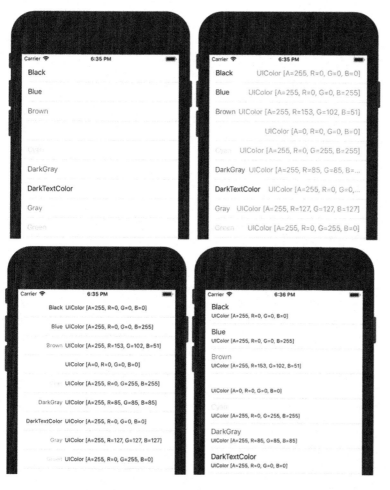

Figure 3-3. *Predefined cell layouts: Default (top left), Value1 (top right), Value2 (bottom left), and Subtitle*

To optimize performance, you typically reuse existing cells with the DequeueReusableCell method of the UITableView class instance. This method accepts the cell identifier and returns either a valid instance of the UITableViewCell or null. In the second case, you need to create a new cell by invoking the UITableViewCell constructor. In Listing 3-7, I use a default cell style and set the cell identifier to that stored in the cellId constant. Given the instance of the UITableViewCell, I configure its properties such that the main label displays a color name while the minor label shows a string representation of the UIColor class instance (type name and ARGB components). Additionally, I change the foreground color of the main label to the color carried by the Value property of the current item. The code from Listing 3-7 depends upon the following namespaces, which you need to include in the ColorsTableSource.cs file:

```
using System;
using System.Collections.Generic;
using Foundation;
using UIKit;
```

Listing 3-7. A Collection of Items for the UITableView

```
public class ColorsTableSource : UITableViewSource
{
    private const string cellId = "ColorCell";

    public List<Color> Items { get; private set; } = ColorsHelper.GetColors();

    public override UITableViewCell GetCell(
        UITableView tableView, NSIndexPath indexPath)
    {
        // Get item to display
        var item = Items[indexPath.Row];

        // Try to reuse a cell before creating the new one
        var cell = tableView.DequeueReusableCell(cellId)
            ?? new UITableViewCell(UITableViewCellStyle.Default, cellId);

        // Configure cell properties
        cell.TextLabel.Text = item.Name;
        cell.TextLabel.TextColor = item.Value;

        if (cell.DetailTextLabel != null)
        {
            cell.DetailTextLabel.Text = item.Value.ToString();
        }

        return cell;
    }

    public override nint RowsInSection(UITableView tableview, nint section)
    {
        return Items.Count;
    }
}
```

Finally, to display a table, I modify the ViewDidLoad method of the ViewController class, as shown in Listing 3-8. First, I instantiate the UITableView class such that it fills the whole view, and then I set its Source property to the instance of the ColorsTableViewSource. Last, I add a table to the view using the Add method of the ViewController class. So, after running the app, you will get the results shown previously in Figure 3-2.

Note that in this example I created the control (UITableView) from the source code. I did not use a visual designer to modify the storyboard. Naturally, you can use this option to define the whole view. In specific cases, this can be faster than designing a view with the storyboard. At the same time, you *can* create the UITableView with a storyboard. In that case, you can manually draw the cell layout and refer to underlying controls by their names.

To successfully compile the code from Listing 3-8, we need to include the ColorsTable.Colors namespace in ViewController.cs file. It is also a good point to stop for a while, compile the app to ensure that everything is working correctly, and test various cell styles.

Listing 3-8. Creating a Table

```
public override void ViewDidLoad()
{
    base.ViewDidLoad();

    var table = new UITableView(View.Frame)
    {
        Source = new ColorsTableSource()
    };

    Add(table);
}
```

Selecting Items

Quite often, you need to display additional data to the user whenever he or she selects an item in the table. Here, I show you how to display the full information about the color (Name and Value) using an alert. You already know how to display an alert, so the only new thing is to create and display the alert from the UITableViewSource whenever the user selects a row. To handle such an event, you override the RowSelected method of the UITableViewSource. The RowSelected method gives you access to a reference to the UITableView, raising an event and an instance of the NSIndexPath class, which you can use to get the index of a selected row. Similarly, as before, I use the index to get the selected item and then create and configure the UIAlertController as shown in Listing 3-9.

Listing 3-9. Displaying Info About Selected Item

```
public override void RowSelected(UITableView tableView, NSIndexPath indexPath)
{
    if (ParentViewController != null)
    {
        DisplayColorInfo(tableView, indexPath);
    }
    else
    {
        base.RowSelected(tableView, indexPath);
    }
}
```

```
private void DisplayColorInfo(UITableView tableView, NSIndexPath indexPath)
{
    var selectedItem = Items[indexPath.Row];

    var alertController = UIAlertController.Create(
        selectedItem.Name, selectedItem.Value.ToString(),
        UIAlertControllerStyle.Alert);

    alertController.AddAction(UIAlertAction.Create(
        "OK", UIAlertActionStyle.Default, null));

    ParentViewController.PresentViewController(
        alertController, true,
          () => { tableView.DeselectRow(indexPath, true); });
}
```

To display an alert, I invoke the PresentViewController method. To do so, I need an instance of the UIViewController or a derived class. Here, I use the ViewController associated with a default view. The ViewController class instance is passed through the constructor of the ColorsTableSource class and then stored in the ParentViewController property (see Listing 3-10).

Listing 3-10. Additional Members of the ColorsTableSource Used to Obtain and Store a Reference to the UIViewController Class

```
public UIViewController ParentViewController { get; private set; }

public ColorsTableSource(UIViewController viewController)
{
    ParentViewController = viewController;
}
```

To use the modified definition of the ColorsTableSource, I change the ViewDidLoad view event handler as shown in Listing 3-11. Afterward, by re-running the app, you can tap any entry in the table. The alert shown in Figure 3-4 appears.

Listing 3-11. Passing an Instance of the ViewController to the ColorsTableSource

```
public override void ViewDidLoad()
{
    base.ViewDidLoad();

    var table = new UITableView(View.Frame)
    {
        Source = new ColorsTableSource(this)
    };

    Add(table);
}
```

Figure 3-4. *Information about the color is displayed as an alert*

Deleting Items

To enable item deletion, override the CommitEditingStyle method of the UITableViewSource. Listing 3-12 shows a sample implementation of this method for the ColorsTableSource. I first read the editingStyle parameter passed to the CommitEditingStyle method to see if it is equal to UITableViewCellEditingStyle. Delete. If so, I remove the selected item from the Colors list and also from the Table View. The latter is done using the DeleteRows method of the UITableView class instance. This method accepts two arguments: an array of NSIndexPath objects, which identify items to be deleted, and animation type. Available animation types are defined in the UITableViewRowAnimation enumeration as follows:

- Fade – specifies that deleted rows will fade out

- Right, Left, Top, Bottom – specify that the deleted rows slide out to the right, left, top, or bottom, respectively

- Middle – specifies that the deleted rows will "fly away"

- Automatic – forces the UITableView to automatically adjust animation style depending on the positions of the rows being deleted

In Listing 3-12, I use Automatic animation, but you can easily change it to any other value and see how it affects row deletion. After running the app, you can choose any item and swipe it to the left; you will see a red *Delete* button (Figure 3-5). After tapping this button, the item will be removed from the underlying list and from the Table View.

Listing 3-12. Deleting an Item

```
public override void CommitEditingStyle(
    UITableView tableView,
    UITableViewCellEditingStyle editingStyle,
    NSIndexPath indexPath)
{
    if (editingStyle == UITableViewCellEditingStyle.Delete)
    {
        Items.RemoveAt(indexPath.Row);
        tableView.DeleteRows(
            new NSIndexPath[] { indexPath },
            UITableViewRowAnimation.Automatic);
    }
}
```

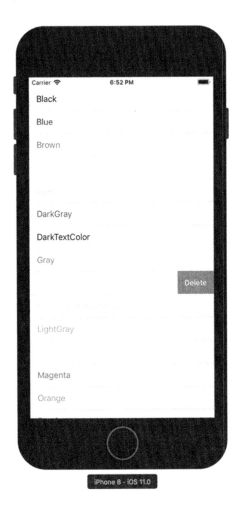

Figure 3-5. *Swipe-to-delete feature in the UITableView*

You can also programmatically prevent an item from being deleted. You do so by implementing the CanEditRow method. Listing 3-13 shows how to prevent deleting a magenta color. When you re-run the app, a *Delete* button will not appear for the row with the magenta color when you swipe the corresponding item.

Listing 3-13. Deleting of the Magenta Color Is Disabled

```
public override bool CanEditRow(UITableView tableView,
    NSIndexPath indexPath)
{
    var itemToDelete = Items[indexPath.Row];

    return itemToDelete.Name != "Magenta";
}
```

In more-advanced scenarios, you may need to create more than one button to handle item swiping. In such cases, you create a collection of UITableViewRowAction objects by overriding the UITableViewRowAction of the UITableViewSource. In Listing 3-14, I implement two such actions. One will look and act analogous to the *Delete* button from the previous example but will have a different label, *Remove*. The other button will have a gray background and will change the background of the selected cell, as shown in Figure 3-6.

Listing 3-14. Creating a Collection of Row Actions

```
public override UITableViewRowAction[] EditActionsForRow(
    UITableView tableView, NSIndexPath indexPath)
{
    var removeButton = UITableViewRowAction.Create(
            UITableViewRowActionStyle.Destructive,
            "Remove",
            delegate {
                Items.RemoveAt(indexPath.Row);
                tableView.DeleteRows(
                    new NSIndexPath[] { indexPath },
                    UITableViewRowAnimation.Middle);
            });

    var markItemButton = UITableViewRowAction.Create(
            UITableViewRowActionStyle.Normal,
            "Mark",
            delegate
            {
                tableView.CellAt(indexPath).BackgroundColor =
                    UIColor.FromRGBA(0, 255, 0, 35);
            });

    return new UITableViewRowAction[] { removeButton, markItemButton };
}
```

To create the `UITableViewRowAction`, you use the static `Create` method. This method accepts three arguments, as follows:

- `style`, which is represented by one of the following values from the `UITableViewRowActionStyle` enumeration:

  - `Default` – specifies that a button will have a default style—red background. Default style is equivalent to Destructive, which means that the button action will remove the item from a table.

  - `Normal` – applies a non-destructive style for a button—gray background

- `Title` – a string you use to set a button label

- `handler` – an action to be invoked after a button is tapped

In Listing 3-14, I use the `UITableViewRowAction.Create` method twice. The resulting two instances of the `UITableViewRowAction` class are used to create an array of row actions. So, every time you swipe a `UITableView` item, two buttons appear, as shown in Figure 3-6. Note that `EditActionsForRow` has higher priority than `CommitEditingStyle`. So, after defining `EditActionsForRow` in the `ColorsTableSource` class, `CommitEditingStyle` is ignored.

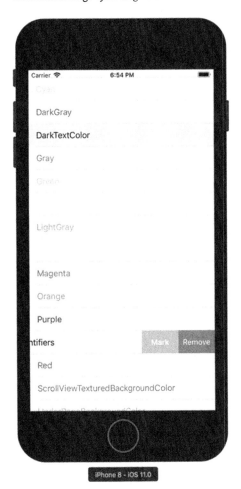

Figure 3-6. *A Table View with two row actions*

60

Web View

A Web View is a visual control that you use to render a web page in your app. A Web View is used in a number of scenarios. For instance, you can use it to display an interactive help guide for your app or to render content from an external server. In this section, I will show you how to build an app that, based on the Web View control, displays a Google Map for a geolocation you choose (Figure 3-7). Note that the Google Map, hosted on a web page rendered in the Web View, will be fully functional. As Figure 3-7 shows, you will be able to translate a map and even enter the street view because Web Views render interactive web pages.

Figure 3-7. *A Web View displaying fully functional Google Maps*

To implement the app shown in Figure 3-7, I use the Single View iOS project template and set the app name to GoogleMap. Then, I create the HTML subfolder, where I put three files: map.css (Listing 3-15), map.js (Listing 3-16), and map.html (Listing 3-17). These files implement a web page that displays two text inputs, one button, and a Google Map. You use input fields to enter latitude and longitude, which are used to set the map's center. The map is displayed when you press a button.

The code of the map.css from Listing 3-15 does not require any additional comments. This is a short definition of the CSS class, named map. This class configures the display mode and dimensions of the resulting map.

Listing 3-15. CSS File Storing a Definition of the map Class

```
.map {
    float: left;
    width: 100%;
    height: 500px;
}
```

The JavaScript function displayMap (map.js) shown in Listing 3-16 is used to display a Google Map in a selected div element. These functions take the geocoordinates for the map's center from two input fields. To this end, displayMap accepts the following three arguments:

- mapDivId – identifier of the div element in which to display a map

- latInputId and lngInputId – identifiers of the input fields with the latitude and longitude, respectively

Given the preceding values, I configure a map options object, which here specifies the zoom and center of the map. Subsequently, I display a map using the google.maps.Map object.

Listing 3-16. JavaScript Function for Displaying a Google Map

```
function displayMap(mapDivId, latInputId, lngInputId) {
    lat = document.getElementById(latInputId).value;
    lng = document.getElementById(lngInputId).value;

    var mapCenter = new google.maps.LatLng(lat, lng);

    var options = {
        zoom: 14,
        center: mapCenter
    };

    new google.maps.Map(document.getElementById(mapDivId), options);
}
```

The last file, for defining a web page, map.html (Listing 3-17), contains a set of standard HTML declarations. Within the head element, I reference a stylesheet, map.css, and necessary JavaScript components. The first one is the Google Map API, while the other is map.js. Then, I declare two labels, two text inputs, a button, and a div element where the map will be rendered. Note that the onclick attribute of the button points to the displayMap function. So, whenever you tap this button, the function from Listing 3-16 will be invoked to display a map.

Listing 3-17. Contents of the map.html File

```
<html>
    <head>
        <link href="map.css" rel="stylesheet" type="text/css"/>
        <script src="https://maps.googleapis.com/maps/api/js"></script>
        <script src="map.js"></script>
    </head>
```

```
<body>
    <p>
        Latitude: <input type="text" id="input-lat"/>
    </p>
    <p>
        Longitude: <input type="text" id="input-lng"/>
    </p>

    <button onclick="displayMap('div-map',
            'input-lat', 'input-lng')">Display map</button>

    <div id="div-map" class="map"/>
</body>
</html>
```

Given the web page is ready, I can now display it using a Web View. To this end, in the `ViewController` class I first import the necessary namespaces:

```
using System;
using System.IO;
using CoreGraphics;
using Foundation;
using UIKit;
```

Then, I define two helper methods, seen in Listing 3-18. The first one, `GetFrameWithVerticalMargin`, is used to determine the rectangle in which I display the Web View. Note that in the previous section, a Table View was overlaid on the status bar. To solve this issue, in Listing 3-18 I add a vertical margin to the rectangle and reduce its height accordingly. The second method, `LoadMapUrl`, invokes the `LoadRequest` method of the `UIWebView` class instance in order to render a web page. `LoadRequest` accepts a single argument of type `NSUrlRequest`. This is instantiated with the `NSUrl` object, pointing to the `map.html` file. So, `UIWebView` will display this web page.

Listing 3-18. Helper Methods Used to Display a Web Page Within the Web View

```
private CGRect GetFrameWithVerticalMargin(nfloat offset)
{
    var rect = View.Frame;

    rect.Y = offset;

    rect.Height -= offset;

    return rect;
}

private void LoadMapUrl(UIWebView webView)
{
    var url = Path.Combine(NSBundle.MainBundle.BundlePath,
        "HTML/map.html");

    webView.LoadRequest(new NSUrlRequest(new NSUrl(url, false)));
}
```

To access the map.html web page during runtime, you need to set the build action of map.css, map.js, and map.html to BundleResource, as shown in Figure 3-8.

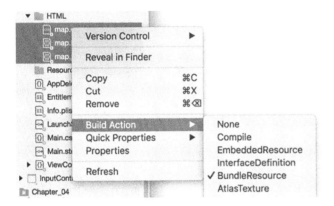

Figure 3-8. *Configuring a build action for the web page*

Lastly, I modify the ViewDidLoad event handler as shown in Listing 3-19. There, I instantiate a Web View control and specify bounds for it using my GetFrameWithVerticalMargin method. Subsequently, I invoke LoadMapUrl and finally display a Web View. So, after you run the app, you will see a web page with text inputs and a button. After entering geocoordinates, you click a button and the map will be displayed after a short while.

Listing 3-19. Creating and Displaying a Web View

```
public override void ViewDidLoad()
{
    base.ViewDidLoad();

    var webView = new UIWebView(GetFrameWithVerticalMargin(20));

    LoadMapUrl(webView);

    Add(webView);
}
```

Google Geocoding API

In the previous sample, I used geocoordinates for New York City. If you would like to display a map for another location, you need to know its geocoordinates. To find these for any address, you can use the Google Geocode service. This is a webservice that converts addresses into geocoordinates (latitude and longitude). To use geocoding, you type the following URL in your browser (you can replace New York with any other value):

https://maps.googleapis.com/maps/api/geocode/json?address=New+York

As a result, the Geocoding API will return the JSON file describing your address. This description is an array of key–value pairs, which store several objects like address components or geometry. In particular, the location of your address is saved under the location key. Here, this key is associated with the following geocoordinates—lat: 40.7127837 and lng: -74.0059413. I used these values to generate screenshots for Figure 3-7. See Listing 3-20.

Listing 3-20. A Sample JSON Response from Google Geocode

```
{
    "results" : [
      {
        "address_components" : [
           {
              "long_name" : "New York",
              "short_name" : "New York",
              "types" : [ "locality", "political" ]
           },
           {
              "long_name" : "New York",
              "short_name" : "NY",
              "types" : [ "administrative_area_level_1", "political" ]
           },
           {
              "long_name" : "United States",
              "short_name" : "US",
              "types" : [ "country", "political" ]
           }
        ],
        "formatted_address" : "New York, NY, USA",
        "geometry" : {
           "bounds" : {
              "northeast" : {
                 "lat" : 40.9175771,
                 "lng" : -73.70027209999999
              },
              "southwest" : {
                 "lat" : 40.4773991,
                 "lng" : -74.25908989999999
              }
           },
           "location" : {
              "lat" : 40.7127837,
              "lng" : -74.0059413
           },
           "location_type" : "APPROXIMATE",
           "viewport" : {
              "northeast" : {
                 "lat" : 40.9152555,
                 "lng" : -73.70027209999999
              },
              "southwest" : {
                 "lat" : 40.4960439,
                 "lng" : -74.25573489999999
              }
           }
        }
      },
```

```
            "place_id" : "ChIJOwg_O6VPwokRYv534QaPC8g",
            "types" : [ "locality", "political" ]
        }
    ], "status" : "OK";
}
```

Invoking JavaScript Functions

A Web View allows you to run JavaScript from the C# code. To that end, Web View delivers the
EvaluateJavaScript method. It accepts one argument, which is a string with JavaScript code to run. To
demonstrate how to use the EvaluateJavascript method, I supplement the map.js file with another
function, displayGeocoordinate (Listing 3-21). This function takes an address, represented as a string, and
displays its geocoordinate, which is obtained from the Google Geocode service (Figure 3-9). To that end,
I instantiate a google.maps.Geocoder object and then invoke its geocode method. This method sends a
request to the Google Geocode service and accepts two arguments. The first one is an array of parameters,
while the second is the callback function, which is executed after the request is completed. A callback
function is fed with two other parameters, as follows:

- results – an object representing the results part of the JSON response from the
  Google Geocode service (refer back to Listing 3-20)

- status – status of the request

In Listing 3-21, I use both parameters. First, I read the status to validate that the request was successfully
handled by Google Geocode. If so, I get the first element of the results array and then obtain the location
from the geometry object.

Listing 3-21. Geocoding an Address

```
function displayGeocoordinate(address) {
    var geocoder = new google.maps.Geocoder();

    geocoder.geocode({'address': address}, function(results, status) {
        if (status === 'OK') {
            var geocoordinate = results[0].geometry.location;

            alert('Address: ' + address
                + '\nLat: ' + geocoordinate.lat().toFixed(3)
                + '\nLng: ' + geocoordinate.lng().toFixed(3));
        }
        else {
            alert('Geocoder failed: ' + status);
        }
    });
}
```

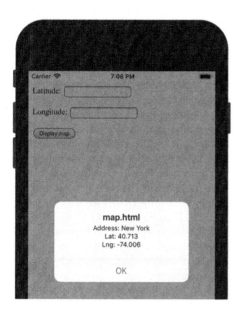

Figure 3-9. *Displaying an alert with a JavaScript function invoked through the Web View*

To invoke the `displayGeocoordinate` function, I modify the `ViewDidLoad` method of the `ViewController` as shown in Listing 3-22. I create the handler for the `LoadFinished` event of the Web View. The latter is fired after the web page has been rendered. This ensures that all necessary references are ready so I can invoke the `displayGeocoordinate` function using `EvaluateJavascript`. For the address, I pass New York, so after re-running an app I obtain the results shown in Figure 3-9. Note that Web View automatically reinterprets the JavaScript alert function such that the resulting popup window looks like the one created with `UIAlertController`.

Listing 3-22. Invoking a JavaScript Function Through the Web View

```
public override void ViewDidLoad()
{
    base.ViewDidLoad();

    var webView = new UIWebView(GetFrameWithVerticalMargin(20));

    LoadMapUrl(webView);

    Add(webView);

    webView.LoadFinished += (sender, e) =>
    {
        webView.EvaluateJavascript("displayGeocoordinate('New York');");
    };
}
```

67

Map View and Geolocation

The goal of the example with the Google Map we developed in the previous section was to show the comprehensive capabilities of the Web View. On iOS, if you want to display a map, you do not necessarily need to use a Web View. Instead, you can use the native map kit, which is delivered by the iOS SDK. In particular, this kit brings the Map View, which you can access through the MKMapView class declared under the MapKit namespace of Xamarin.iOS. MKMapView lets you quickly add an interactive native iOS map to your app. In this map, you can even display the current location of the user's device, add appropriate annotations, or even display driving directions. Accordingly, you can relatively quickly add advanced functionality to your app. In this section, I will tell you how to use the map kit along with the CLLocationManager, a class used to track the geolocation of the iOS device, to create an app that will display the user's location on the map. More specifically, the app will have a single view, which will look like the one from Figure 3-10.

To implement this app, I start by creating a new project with the Single View App template. I set the app name and its minimum target version to Map and iOS 9.0, respectively. Then, in the ViewController class, I import three namespaces: MapKit, System.Linq, and CoreLocation. Subsequently, I declare the private member, map, and a helper function, InitMap (Listing 3-23). This method is used to create an instance of the MKMapView class and set its selected properties. Specifically, I enable zooming and scrolling and set the ShowsUserLocation property to true. This enables a map to display the user's location, which is indicated by the blue dot with a white border (Figure 3-10). Additionally, I configure the map type using the corresponding property of the MKMapView class instance. All available map types are defined under the MKMapType enumeration. You can choose between the following map styles:

- Standard – indicates that a map uses standard cartographic map style (similar to the one shown in left part of Figure 3-7)

- Satellite – a map will be created using images acquired with a satellite

- Hybrid – a combination of standard and satellite images

- SatelliteFlyover and HybridFlyovers – indicate that a map type will be a flyover of the satellite or hybrid imaginary, respectively

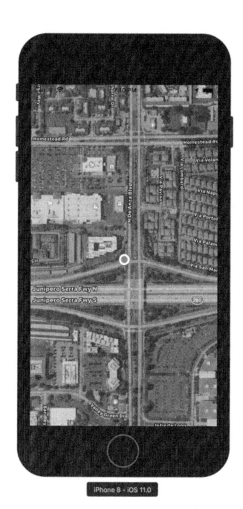

Figure 3-10. *Exemplary use of the map view*

Listing 3-23. Initializing a Map

```
private MKMapView map;

private void InitMap()
{
    map = new MKMapView(View.Frame)
    {
        ZoomEnabled = true,
        ScrollEnabled = true,
        MapType = MKMapType.HybridFlyover,
        ShowsUserLocation = true
    };

    Add(map);
}
```

To display a map, you add the InitMap method to the ViewDidLoad event handler of the ViewController class. If you do so and re-run the app, you will see that the view will be filled with a map view. You can arbitrarily translate the map view. If you want to zoom the map view in the simulator, then you would need to press and hold the Alt/Option key. Two circles, representing two fingers, will be shown in the simulator. They emulate the positions of your fingers during the pinch gesture. So, you can now change a distance between circles to increase or decrease the map zoom.

Listing 3-24. Instantiating CLLocationManager

```
private CLLocationManager locationManager;

private void InitLocationManager()
{
    locationManager = new CLLocationManager();

    // Request authorization
    if (UIDevice.CurrentDevice.CheckSystemVersion(8, 0))
    {
        locationManager.RequestWhenInUseAuthorization();
    }

    // Handle LocationsUpdated event
    locationManager.LocationsUpdated += (sender, e) =>
    {
        UpdateMap(e);
    };
}
```

Let's now move forward and access the device's geolocation. To that end, I extend a definition of the ViewController class by another private field, locationManager, of the CLLocationManager and a helper method, InitLocationManager (Listing 3-24). This method creates an instance of the CLLocationManager with the default parameterless constructor and then requests that the user allow the Map app to access his location when the app is running in the foreground. To this end, I use the RequestWhenInUseAuthorization. If you want to access the device's location in the background also, then you need to use the RequestAlwaysAuthorization method. Independently of the method you choose, you also need to specify a corresponding property in the Information property list. You configure this under the Source tab of the Info.plist editor (refer back to Chapter 2). Then, you click the "Add new entry" link (the last element of the list); a custom property string appears. Next to it, you will find an icon, which activates the drop-down list. You use this list to choose "Location When In Use Usage Description" (foreground access to user's location) or "Location Always Usage Description" (background access to user's location). Here, I use the first property (Figure 3-11). Then, in the Value column of the editor, you type the string. This string defines a message that will be displayed to the user whose location you request to access. This modal window is displayed automatically whenever you invoke RequestWhenInUseAuthorization (Figure 3-12) and your app does not have access to the user's location.

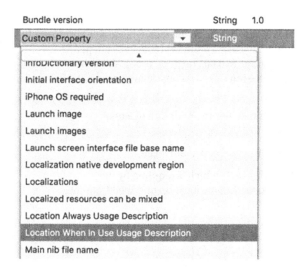

| Bundle version | String | 1.0 |
| Custom Property ▼ | String | |

InfroDictionary version

Initial interface orientation

iPhone OS required

Launch image

Launch images

Launch screen interface file base name

Localization native development region

Localizations

Localized resources can be mixed

Location Always Usage Description

Location When In Use Usage Description

Main nib file name

Figure 3-11. *Adding a custom property to the Information property list*

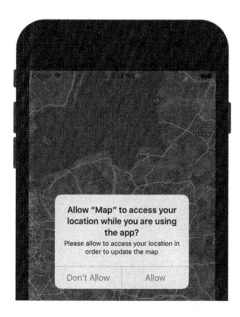

Allow "Map" to access your location while you are using the app?

Please allow to access your location in order to update the map

Don't Allow   Allow

Figure 3-12. *Requesting access to user's location*

You can request the user's private data only in iOS 8.0 or above. Therefore, before I invoke RequestWhenInUseAuthorization, I verify the iOS version using the CheckSystemVersion method of the CurrentDevice static property of the UIDevice class.

Finally, in Listing 3-24, I associate the UpdateMap method with the LocationsUpdated event handler of the CLLocationManager class instance. The LocationsUpdated event is fired whenever the user's location changes. A definition of the UpdateMap and its dependencies is given in Listing 3-25. As shown there, I first read the last known location and use it to set the map center and configure a map region. The latter is the fragment of a map that is displayed or defines the map zoom. To configure a map region, I first create an instance of the MKCoordinateSpan class. You use this class to specify the map distance for latitude (north to south) and longitude (east to west) using corresponding arguments (latitudeDelta and longitudeDelta) of the MKCoordinateSpan class constructor. Both arguments are expressed in degrees. One degree corresponds to approximately 69 miles (111 kilometers). However, an exact value for the latitudeDelta depends on the longitudinal span. Here, I set the span for both directions to 0.005 degrees. Given an instance of MKCoordinateSpan, I use it to instantiate the MKCoordinateRegion class. Its constructor accepts the following two arguments:

- center of type CLLocationCoordinate2D, which specifies the midpoint of a map region

- span of type MKCoordinateSpan, which determines the map zoom level

In order to obtain an instance of the CLLocationCoordinate2D, which is required by the MKCoordinateRegion constructor, I read the Coordinate property of the location obtained from the CLLocationManager (Listing 3-25).

Listing 3-25. Updating a Map View to Display User's Location

```
private const double spanDelta = 0.005d;

private void UpdateMap(CLLocationsUpdatedEventArgs e)
{
    var location = e.Locations.LastOrDefault();

    if (location != null)
    {
        map.CenterCoordinate = location.Coordinate;

        SetMapRegion(location.Coordinate);
    }
}

private void SetMapRegion(CLLocationCoordinate2D centerCoordinate)
{
    var span = new MKCoordinateSpan(spanDelta, spanDelta);

    var region = new MKCoordinateRegion(centerCoordinate, span);

    map.SetRegion(region, false);
}
```

Lastly, I add the InitLocationManager method to ViewDidLoad (Listing 3-26). Then, I need to force CLLocationManager to report changes in the user's location. To this end, I invoke the StartUpdatingLocation method within the ViewDidAppear view event handler. Correspondingly, when the view disappears I invoke StopUpdatingLocation so the app does not access the user's location when running in the background.

You can now you re-run the app, and you will quickly see that the map view displays the user's current location. To emulate changes in geoposition within the simulator, you can use several options from the simulator's Debug/Location menu (Figure 3-13). You will achieve the best results with City Bicycle Ride, City Run, or Freeway Drive.

Listing 3-26. View Event Handlers of the ViewController

```
public override void ViewDidLoad()
{
    base.ViewDidLoad();

    InitMap();

    InitLocationManager();
}

public override void ViewDidAppear(bool animated)
{
    locationManager.StartUpdatingLocation();
}

public override void ViewDidDisappear(bool animated)
{
    base.ViewDidDisappear(animated);

    locationManager.StopUpdatingLocation();
}
```

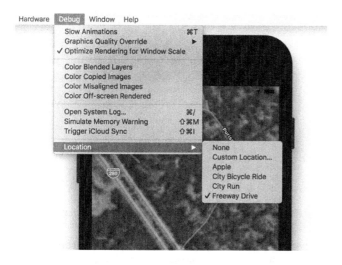

Figure 3-13. A screenshot showing Location menu you can use to emulate changes in geolocation of the simulator

Auto-Layout

Creating adaptive views or auto-layout is one of the biggest challenges in mobile development. Controls of the adaptive view have to be automatically resized or rearranged to fit the available space when the view is resized or rotated. To design such an auto-layout, you utilize a platform-specific mechanism to automatically adjust the view layout to the device's screen size.

To formulate a problem to be tackled by the auto-layout, I use a direct example. To that end, I create a new single view, universal iOS app targeting iOS 9.0 and above. I set the app name to AutoLayout and then go to the iOS designer, where I first choose iPhone 6 from the View As drop-down list (Figure 3-14). Then, I add one label and one text field to the view of the ViewController. I set the label text to *First name:* and put it right above the text field. I set fixed widths for the label and text field to 90 and 355 px, respectively. So, in the iOS designer, my layout looks fine on the iPhone 6 (Figure 3-14).

Figure 3-14. *iOS designer showing the preview of AutoLayout app on iPhone 6*

When I change the iOS designer preview to iPhone 5[S], the text field becomes clipped (see top part of Figure 3-15). A contrary problem occurs on devices with larger screens; e.g., on iPhone 6 Plus, my text field becomes too short (bottom part of Figure 3-15).

Figure 3-15. *Preview of the AutoLayout app on the iPhone 5S and iPhone 6 Plus reveals layout issues*

The preceding problem can be fixed with the use of *constraints*. They define a set of rules that are used by the runtime to automatically resize or rearrange the controls of the particular view. For instance, you can define margins between a text field and screen bounds such that the width of a text field will be automatically changed to fit the available space. To define such constraints, you use the iOS designer, where you click the text field twice (do not double-click the control). As Figure 3-16 shows, the text field becomes surrounded by four T symbols, which represent pin spacing (distance between controls), and two double-T symbols, used to specify pin sizing (sizes of controls).

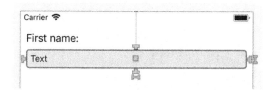

Figure 3-16. *T-shaped and double T-shaped icons can be used to visually define constraints*

Now, click and hold the T-shape located on the right-hand side of the text field. A dashed green line appears on the right (Figure 3-17). This line represents a default margin. You can drag the T-shape to define the constraint. Let's move it above the green dashed line, and then, as shown in the bottom part of Figure 3-17, release the mouse button after the color of the dashed line changes to blue. Visual Studio creates the first constraint and displays a yellow warning sign in the bottom of the View Controller rectangle. After you click it, a message appears, telling you to add another constraint for the Y position (Figure 3-18). To do so, just click the *Update Constraints* button. Finally, click the T-shaped icon to the left of the text field and drag it over the green dashed line located on the left-hand side of the view (similar to what you did with the left margin). You should now have three constraints for a text field. To see a list of constraints, use the Layout tab of the text field properties window (Figure 3-19).

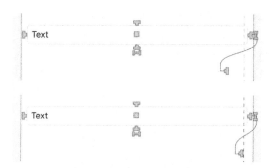

Figure 3-17. *Creating a spacing constraint*

Figure 3-18. *Updating constraints*

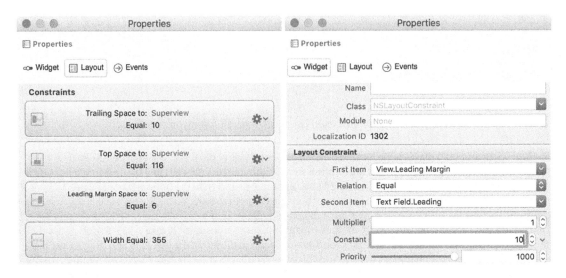

Figure 3-19. *Constraints can be edited using the Properties window*

As Figure 3-19 shows, the list of constraints is displayed under the group of the same name. In this case, I have four constraints, as follows:

- Trailing Space to: Superview, equal to: 10 – specifies the right margin between text field and a superview

- Top Space to: Superview, equal to: 116 – specifies a top margin between text field and a superview

- Leading Margin Space to: Superview, equal to: 6 – this constraint specifies a left margin between text field and a superview, the view in which text field is embedded

- Width equal to 355 – specifies width of the text field. This constraint was generated to reflect the initial width we set at the beginning of implementation.

Note that each entry of the constraints group has a small icon that graphically represents a constraint (on the left), and also a settings drop-down list (on the right). You use the latter to either delete or edit the constraint. Deleting a constraint does not warrant additional comment, unlike the edit mode. Once in the editing mode (right part of Figure 3-19), you can modify the multiplier and constant of the constraint. These values are used by the runtime to resize a control according to the mathematical formula: [attribute of the first item] = [attribute of the second item] × Multiplier + Constant. You can change this equality to an inequality with a Relation drop-down list. This has three available options: Equal (=), LessThanOrEqual (<=), and GreaterThanOrEqual (>=).

I can now modify the Leading Margin Space to 10 and Top Space to 60 px, respectively. Also, the last constraint (Width Equal to 355 px) will cause conflicts when the screen size changes since the layout mechanism cannot satisfy this constraint. Therefore, I remove this constraint. All remaining constraints ensure that a text field will have a fixed margin. So, when the screen size changes, the width of the text field will be updated as follows: [width of the text field] = [width of the view] – 2 × 10. Let's check this and change the preview to smaller (iPhone 5[S]) and larger (iPhone 6 Plus) devices. In both cases, the text field fits the view as in the case of iPhone 6 because it is auto-layouted.

Size Classes

Although the text field of the AutoLayout app adjusts to the screen width, it will disappear when you change the preview to iPad or switch the device orientation from portrait to landscape. This is because portrait orientation uses a different size class than landscape uses. Figure 3-20 shows that iPhone 5[S] in portrait mode utilizes a **w**Compact**h**Regular size class, contrary to the **w**Compact**h**Compact class used in landscape mode.

Figure 3-20. *Size classes for various orientations of iPhone 5S*

A size class specifies the group of devices and their orientation for which the available view sizes have a similar width and height. There are three different classes for width (**w**) and height (**h**):

- Any – a group of devices with screens of arbitrary width or height. This is the most general group, covering all devices.

- Regular – represents devices of regular screen sizes

- Compact – represents devices with compact screens

Accordingly, you can arrange 3 × 3 combinations of these classes, resulting in nine size classes total, which are summarized in Table 3-1. To see how devices are categorized into size classes, click the class name, located to the left of the View As drop-down list. A small popup window appears. This window is partitioned into a 3 × 3 grid. By moving a pointer within this grid, various cells are highlighted, describing the size class. Its description and covered devices are then displayed in the bottom (Figure 3-21).

Table 3-1. *Size Classes for iOS Apps*

Width/Height	Any	Regular	Compact
Any	wAnyhAny	wAnyhR	wAnyhC
Regular	wRhAny	wRhR	wRhC
Compact	wChAny	wChR	wChC

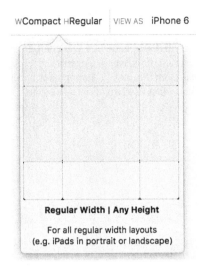

wCompact HRegular   VIEW AS   iPhone 6

Regular Width | Any Height

For all regular width layouts
(e.g. iPads in portrait or landscape)

Figure 3-21. *A grid showing size class along with its short description*

When you use iOS designer to design a view, the controls you add are implicitly associated with the actual size class. So, when you change the size class, these controls do not appear. The only exception is the **wAnyhAny** class, which is associated with the Generic device from the View As drop-down list. In this case, the layout you define will work the same for every device and orientation.

You may wonder why you need size classes. The simplest answer is that they allow you to easily design adaptive views. For instance, the layout I use in the AutoLayout app works perfectly for portrait mode. The label is above the text field, so the user can easily modify the text. However, when the device orientation is changed to landscape, the text field would be resized to fit the available width, but this will not look natural. Instead, it would be more efficient to change the layout and place the label to the left of the text field. By doing so you will save the vertical space for other controls and use the available space more efficiently.

Let's see how to implement such a dynamic change of control arrangement. I start by installing the wChC class for the text field and the label. To this end, I use the Properties window, in which the list of installed size classes is located right below the Height property (Figure 3-22). Then, I click the Settings drop-down list and choose the Compact ➤ Compact option from the context menu. The first specifies the width group, while the second corresponds to the height group.

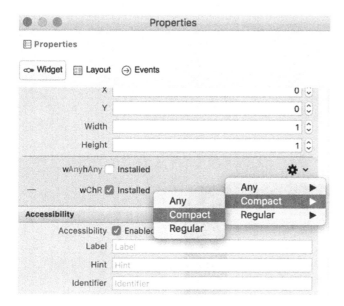

Figure 3-22. *Installing the wChC size class*

Given the new size classes are installed, I can switch the preview mode to landscape. The controls become visible. However, the width of the text field does not change, because constraints I defined previously work for the **wChR** size class only. I need to specify new constraints for the **wChC** size class. I can also arbitrarily rearrange controls. So, I first place the text field next to the label. Then, analogously as for the **wChR** size class, I use a T-shaped icons to define three constraints between the text field and the superview (parent view) such that the left, top, and right margins are fixed to 100, 32, and 10 px, respectively. You add these constraints analogously as previously, with the only difference being that now you need to drag the left T-shape to the text field. After defining new constraints for the **wChC** size class, I re-run the AutoLayout app, and its view now depends on the screen orientation (Figure 3-23).

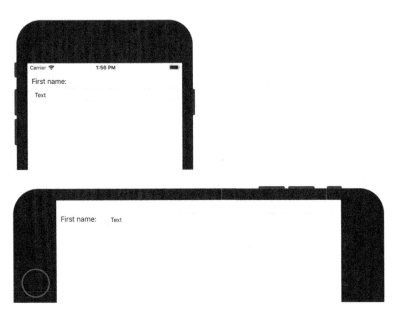

Figure 3-23. *AutoLayout, when combined with the size classes, allows you to design adaptive views in which the controls are resized and rearranged according to screen-size orientation: portrait (top) and landscape (bottom)*

UI Thread

In many scenarios, you need to update specific properties of the controls from a background thread to avoid blocking the user interface, which is controlled by the main or UI thread. For instance, when the user presses a button, you send a request to a web service and wait for a response and update the UI accordingly. Depending on the network speed, this can take from a few to several seconds. So, the UI can freeze for a while. To avoid such locks, you need to send and parse a request in the background thread. However, as every Xamarin.iOS app utilizes the .NET Framework, you need to ensure that all updates to visual controls are performed from the UI thread. This is required by the .NET threading model, in which only the UI thread can access visual controls. In .NET Framework apps, when you try to update visual controls from the background thread, a corresponding exception is thrown. Let's investigate this issue in a Xamarin.iOS app. To this end, I create another app, BackgroundUpdate (Single View App project template, targeting iOS 9.0 and above). Then, I define the user interface of this app such that the default view contains a button with caption *Run timer* and a label named LabelTime. A button is located on top, while the label is placed below it. Then, I create a default event handler for the button and define it according to Listing 3-27. This code requires a System.Threading.Tasks namespace.

When the user presses a button, I run another method, UpdateTimer, in a background thread using the static Run method of the Task class. This method enqueues the specified block of code to be executed in the *thread pool*. The thread pool is a set of pre-created background threads. They are created by the runtime in order to save time when executing work in the background.

Listing 3-27. Enqueueing UpdateTimer Method in the Thread Pool

```
private bool isTimerActive = false;

partial void ButtonRunTimer_TouchUpInside(UIButton sender)
{
    if (!isTimerActive)
    {
        isTimerActive = true;

        Task.Run(UpdateTimer);
    }
}
```

As shown in Listing 3-28, the UpdateTimer implements an infinite loop. At each iteration of this loop, I read the current time and rewrite it to the Text property of the LabelTime. Then, I delay execution of the loop by a one-second (Task.Delay). Therefore, I expect that UpdateTimer will work like a simple watch and display a current time with one-second accuracy. However, when I run the app in the simulator and press a button, nothing happens, although the UpdateTimer method is running. The application output shows the reason for that: *UIKit Consistency error: you are calling a UIKit method that can only be invoked from the UI thread.* This means that you cannot update visual controls from the background thread directly. Instead, you need to invoke every such operation on the main thread. To do so, you use the InvokeOnMainThread method as shown in Listing 3-29. After making these changes in the UpdateTimer method, the timer will work correctly after you re-run the app (Figure 3-24).

Listing 3-28. Updating Text Property of the Label from the Background Thread Does Not Work

```
private Task UpdateTimer()
{
    while (true)
    {
        try
        {
            LabelTime.Text = DateTime.Now.ToLongTimeString();
        }
        catch(Exception e)
        {
            Console.WriteLine(e.Message);
        }

        Task.Delay(1000).Wait();
    }
}
```

Listing 3-29. Properties of Visual Controls Can Be Updated from the Main Thread Only

```
private Task UpdateTimer()
{
    while (true)
    {
```

```
        InvokeOnMainThread(() =>
        {
            LabelTime.Text = DateTime.Now.ToLongTimeString();
        });

        Task.Delay(1000).Wait();
    }
}
```

Figure 3-24. *Exemplary results of the BackgroundUpdate app*

Summary

In this chapter, you learned how to define views. We started by creating single view applications in order to master the use of some basic controls like switch or slider. Then, we moved to the more advanced topics of using tables and their sources to create views, which display multiple items. You also learned how to render interactive web pages using the Web View, and to access and display the user's location using the map kit. Subsequently, we worked with auto-layouts, which you can use to design adaptive apps, whose views adjust automatically to the particular device's size. In the next chapter, we will continue to work with views. Namely, we will create multi-view applications and learn how to navigate between views using various navigation approaches.

■ ■ ■

CHAPTER 4

Navigation

In all previous samples, we created single view apps. However, in practice your app will most likely comprise more than one view. To implement such a multi-view app you need to know how to handle navigation, which is defined as switching between the views. In this section, I will discuss several approaches for creating multi-view apps.

Tab Bar

I start with the tab bar control, which lets you create multi-tab apps. In this case, the user switches between various views (tabs) using a bar. This bar contains buttons with icons and optional labels. When the user presses such a button, a corresponding tab appears.

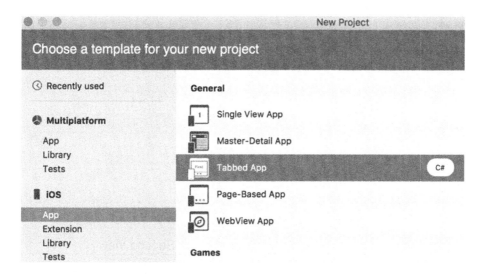

Figure 4-1. *Creating a tabbed app in Visual Studio*

To create the tabbed app, I use a dedicated project template (see Figure 4-1). I set the app name to *Navigation.Tabs* and the minimum target version to iOS 9.0. Visual Studio creates a project comprising the following view controllers (see Figure 4-2):

- Tab Bar Controller – the controller that manages the tab interface. More specifically, this controller is responsible for switching between tabs. Each tab has separate view controllers and corresponding views.

- First View Controller and Second View Controller – view controllers associated with the first and second tabs. Note that the Navigation.Tabs project also contains two files: `FirstViewController.cs` and `SecondViewController.cs`, which store definitions of the classes of the same names. `FirstViewController` and `SecondViewController` both derive from the `UIViewController` and, apart from the protected constructor, contain default implementations of the `ViewDidLoad` and `DidReceiveMemoryWarning` methods, similar to the definition of the `ViewController` class utilized in all previous single view apps.

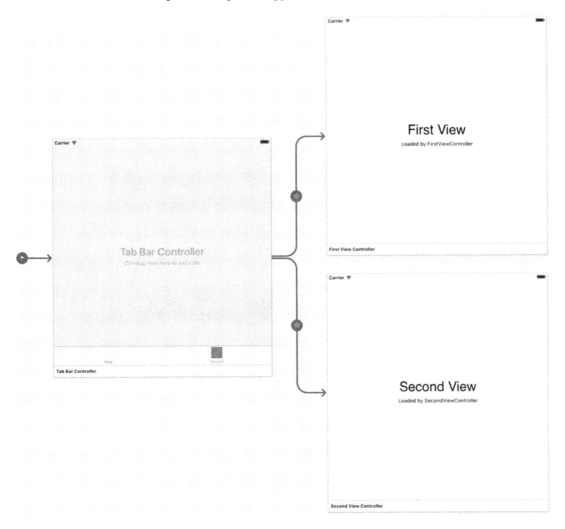

Figure 4-2. A default structure of the tabbed app created from a dedicated template

Note that by default there are only two tabs, so when you run the app it will look as shown in Figure 4-3. Namely, the bar has two elements: First and Second. You can tap them to switch between tabs. Each tab has two labels, which display the view number and the name of the associated class implementing the view controller.

Figure 4-3. *A default tabbed app*

To control the appearance of an item in the tab bar, you use the properties of the tab bar item. As the left part of Figure 4-4 shows (Document Outline), each tab has an associated tab bar item. When you click it, all control properties appear under the Properties pad (right part of Figure 4-4). In particular, you can modify the item title (Title entry under Bar Item group) and its image (drop-down list right below Title). You can also use one of the system icons via the System Item drop-down list (Tab Bar Item group). This list includes the following tab bar icons: bookmarks, contacts, downloads, favorites, featured, history, more, most recent, most viewed, recents, search, and top rated.

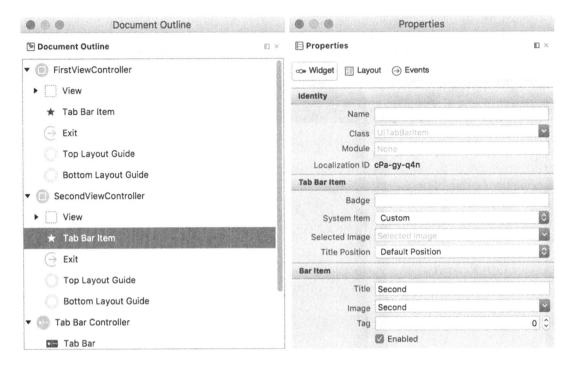

Figure 4-4. *The properties pad of the selected tab bar item*

Now that we know the structure of the Navigation.Tabs project, let's see how to add another tab. To this end, I proceed as follows. First, in the iOS designer, I add the view controller from the Toolbox. Then, I associate this object with the tab bar controller using CTRL+Drag. I click the gray area of the tab bar controller while pressing CTRL on the keyboard. Then, I move the mouse cursor on the new view controller and release the mouse button. A segue popup appears from which I choose Tab under the Relationship group (Figure 4-5).

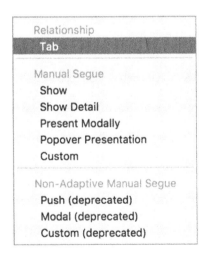

Figure 4-5. *Creating a tab relationship*

iOS designer creates the third tab, which I can now design by modifying the view of the new view controller. Lastly, I create the view controller class. To this end, I use the Properties pad of the view controller, where under the Identity group I type *ThirdViewController* in the Class entry (Figure 4-6). After pressing Enter, Visual Studio adds the `ThirdViewController.cs` file to the Navigation.Tabs project.

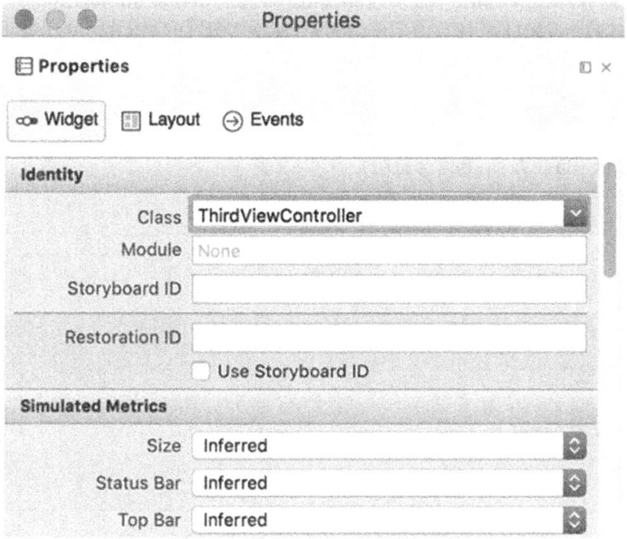

Figure 4-6. *Associating a class with the view controller*

Before I implement the `ThirdViewController` class, I add to the project another file, `BaseViewController.cs`, in which I define a base class for all other view controllers (Listing 4-1). I use the base class because I want all my view controllers to follow a similar logic whenever the associated view appears. Namely, I display in the application output the name of the class associated with the view. I implement such a logic to explicitly show you that different views are displayed when you switch between tabs. Therefore, you can use this option to write custom logic that handles the view lifecycle for tabs just as you can for all other views.

Listing 4-1. Displaying the Name of a Type Associated with the View When the View Is About to Appear

```
using System;
using System.Diagnostics;
using Foundation;
using UIKit;

namespace Navigation.Tabs
{
    public class BaseViewController : UIViewController
    {
        protected BaseViewController(IntPtr handle) : base(handle) { }

        public override void ViewWillAppear(bool animated)
        {
            base.ViewDidLoad();
```

```
            Debug.WriteLine(GetType().Name);
        }
    }
}
```

Given the BaseViewController, I create the skeleton of the ThirdViewController class as shown in Listing 4-2 and modify declarations of the FirstViewController and SecondViewController such that they derive from BaseViewController instead of from UIViewController (Listing 4-3).

Listing 4-2. A Skeleton of the ThirdViewController Class

```
public partial class ThirdViewController : BaseViewController
{
    public ThirdViewController(IntPtr handle) : base(handle) { }

    public override void ViewDidLoad()
    {
        base.ViewDidLoad();
    }

    public override void DidReceiveMemoryWarning()
    {
        base.DidReceiveMemoryWarning();
    }
}
```

Listing 4-3. Modified Declarations of the FirstViewController and the SecondViewController

```
public partial class FirstViewController : BaseViewController

public partial class SecondViewController : BaseViewController
```

The preceding changes ensure that when you run the app and switch between tabs you will see the class name in the application output. However, when you activate the last tab, it will be empty, and also the last tab bar item will display a default button. To change the icon and the caption of the tab bar item I use the Properties pad (refer back to Figure 4-4), where I select the More icon from the System Item drop-down list. To add a label on the last tab, I open the ThirdViewController.cs file and define the AddLabel method. Lastly, I invoke this method in the ViewDidLoad view event handler (Listing 4-4).

Listing 4-4. Creating a Label Dynamically

```
public override void ViewDidLoad()
{
    base.ViewDidLoad();

    AddLabel();
}
```

```
private void AddLabel()
{
    // Create the label
    var label = new UILabel()
    {
        Text = "Third View"
    };

    // Update font size
    nfloat fontSize = 36.0f;
    label.Font = label.Font.WithSize(fontSize);

    // Measure the label
    var labelSize = UIStringDrawing.StringSize(label.Text, label.Font);

    // and adjust the frame accordingly
    label.Frame = new CGRect(View.Frame.Width / 2 - labelSize.Width / 2,
                      View.Frame.Height / 2 - labelSize.Height / 2,
                      labelSize.Width,
                      labelSize.Height) ;

    Add(label);
}
```

In the AddLabel method, I first instantiate the UILabel class and set its Text property to Third View. Subsequently, I set the font size to 36 pixels and measure the resulting label with the static method StringSize of the UIStringDrawing class. This method returns an instance of the CGRect class, which I use to set the position of the label such that it is centered within the view. Then, I invoke the Add method of the UIViewController class to add the label to the view. I also change the button for the third bar to More by modifying the appropriate property of the tab bar item of the last tab (refer back to Figure 4-3). So, after re-running the app, it will look as shown in Figure 4-7.

Figure 4-7. *The final form of the Navigation.Tabs app*

Pages

There is yet another project template, which enables you to jumpstart implementing multi-view apps—the Page-Based App template, highlighted in Figure 4-8. In this section, I will use this template to create another app, *Navigation.PageBased*, which targets iOS 9.0 and above. When you use this template, Visual Studio creates the app, which has twelve pages, each of which displays the name of the month in the label. So, when you run the app, it will look as shown in Figure 4-9.

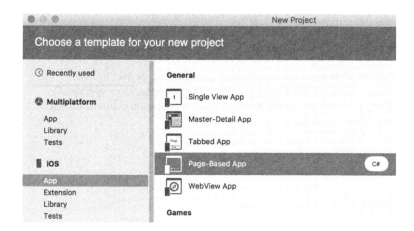

Figure 4-8. New Project window, showing Page-Based App iOS project template

Figure 4-9. A default page-based application has twelve pages, each of which displays a month name

Let's see how the Navigation.PageBased app works. If you open the iOS designer of this project, you will see that it is composed of the two controllers:

- Root View Controller – the initial view controller, that provides content view of the windows,

- Data View Controller – a view controller that provides and displays data (appropriate month name) at each page.

The logic for the root view controller is implemented within the class of the same name and stored under the RootViewController.cs file. RootViewController has two public members (Listing 4-5): ModelController and PageViewController.

Listing 4-5. Public Members of the RootViewController

```
public UIPageViewController PageViewController { get; private set; }

public ModelController ModelController { get; private set; }
```

The first member, PageViewController, is of type UIPageViewController. The latter represents the page view controller. This controller is the central part of the Navigation.PageBased project (and all other projects created with the Page-Based App template) and manages the navigation between the

91

underlying pages. Each of these pages has an associated view controller, which in this case is represented as the DataViewController class. The PageViewController is instantiated within the ViewDidLoad event handler of the RootViewController (see companion code, Chapter_04/Navigation.PageBased/ RootViewController.cs).

The second public member of the RootViewController, the ModelController, derives from the UIPageViewControllerDataSource class and implements a data source for each page. More specifically, ModelController has a pageData field, which is the collection of strings. This collection contains the list of months, which is obtained using the NSDateFormatter class (Listing 4-6).

Listing 4-6. Fragment of the ModelController Class Definition

```
public class ModelController : UIPageViewControllerDataSource
{
    readonly List<string> pageData;

    public ModelController()
    {
        var formatter = new NSDateFormatter();
        pageData = new List<string>(formatter.MonthSymbols);
    }

    // The rest of ModelController definition
}
```

Then, the ModelController implements a GetViewController method, which is shown in Listing 4-7. GetViewController creates an instance of the DataViewController using the InstantiateViewController static method of the UIStoryboard class instance. Subsequently, GetViewController passes an appropriate month name to the created view controller. The month name is stored in the DataObject public property of the DataViewController class instance.

Listing 4-7. GetViewController Method of the ModelController Class

```
public DataViewController GetViewController(int index, UIStoryboard storyboard)
{
    if (index >= pageData.Count)
        return null;

    // Create a new view controller and pass suitable data.
    var dataViewController = (DataViewController)storyboard.
        InstantiateViewController("DataViewController");

    dataViewController.DataObject = pageData[index];

    return dataViewController;
}
```

The GetViewController method is utilized in GetNextViewController and GetPreviousViewController, being overrides of the corresponding methods from the base class, UIPageViewControllerDataSource (see Listing 4-8). These two methods are invoked when the user switches between tabs, so the month name is displayed through the DataViewController.

Listing 4-8. Implementation of the GetNextViewController and GetPreviousViewController of the UIPageViewControllerDataSource Class

```
public override UIViewController GetNextViewController(
    UIPageViewController pageViewController,
    UIViewController referenceViewController)
{
    int index = IndexOf((DataViewController)referenceViewController);

    if (index == -1 || index == pageData.Count - 1)
        return null;

    return GetViewController(index + 1, referenceViewController.Storyboard);
}

public override UIViewController GetPreviousViewController (
    UIPageViewController pageViewController,
    UIViewController referenceViewController)
{
    int index = IndexOf((DataViewController) referenceceViewController);

    if (index == -1 || index == 0)
        return null;

    return GetViewController(index - 1, referenceViewController.Storyboard);
}

public int IndexOf(DataViewController viewController)
{
    return pageData.IndexOf(viewController.DataObject);
}
```

As I mentioned previously, the `DataViewController` class has one public member, `DataObject`. It is used to pass the month name. Then, this value is displayed in the label, identified as `dataLabel`, whenever the view is about to appear (Listing 4-9).

Listing 4-9. A Definition of the DataViewController Class

```
public partial class DataViewController : UIViewController
{
    public string DataObject

    protected DataViewController(IntPtr handle) : base(handle) { }

    // Default definitions of the ViewDidLoad
    // and DidReceiveMemoryWarning

    public override void ViewWillAppear(bool animated)
    {
        base.ViewWillAppear(animated);
        dataLabel.Text = DataObject;
    }
}
```

After getting to know the structure of the Navigation.Pages project, let's modify it. I will now replace the default data source, the list of months, by a list of key-value pairs. Each such pair will consist of a color caption and an instance of the UIColor class. The color caption will be displayed in the label, replacing the month name, while an instance of the UIColor will be used to set the background of the page, as shown in Figure 4-10.

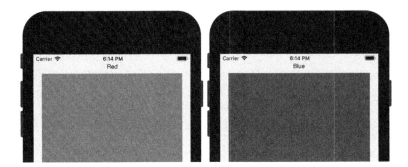

Figure 4-10. *A modified page-based app now displays names of colors instead of months. Moreover, the background color of the rectangle corresponds to the color name displayed in the label.*

To introduce the preceding changes, I first open the iOS designer, then set the name of the white rectangle from the data view controller to ViewDataPanel. Then, I modify the DataViewController class according to Listing 4-10.

Listing 4-10. A Modified Definition of the DataViewController Class

```
using System;
using System.Collections.Generic;
using UIKit;

namespace Navigation.PageBased
{
    public partial class DataViewController : UIViewController
    {
        public KeyValuePair<string, UIColor> DataObject { get; set; }

        protected DataViewController(IntPtr handle) : base(handle) { }

        // Default definitions of ViewDidLoad
        // and DidReceiveMemoryWarning

        public override void ViewWillAppear(bool animated)
        {
            base.ViewWillAppear(animated);

            dataLabel.Text = DataObject.Key;
            ViewDataPanel.BackgroundColor = DataObject.Value;
        }
    }
}
```

In Listing 4-10, I replaced the type of the DataObject member from string to KeyValuePair<string, UIColor>. Then, in the ViewWillAppear view event handler, I obtain the color name and value from the Key and Value properties of DataObject, respectively.

Lastly, I need to update the ModelController, in which I change the declaration and initialization of the pageData member as shown in Listing 4-11. I create three KeyValuePair objects:

- Key: *Red*, Value: UIColor.Red

- Key: *Green*, Value: UIColor.Green

- Key: *Blue*, Value: UIColor.Blue

So, when you re-run the app, there will be three pages available, each of which will correspond to an appropriate color (red, green, or blue). Therefore, the app will look as previously shown in Figure 4-10.

Listing 4-11. A Modified Data Source for the Page View Controller

```
public class ModelController : UIPageViewControllerDataSource
{
    readonly List<KeyValuePair<string, UIColor>> pageData;

    public ModelController()
    {
        pageData = new List<KeyValuePair<string, UIColor>>
        {
            new KeyValuePair<string, UIColor>("Red", UIColor.Red),
            new KeyValuePair<string, UIColor>("Green", UIColor.Green),
            new KeyValuePair<string, UIColor>("Blue", UIColor.Blue)
        };
    }

    // The rest of ModelController definition
}
```

Navigation Between View Controllers

Although tabbed and page-based project templates can be utilized to quickly create multi-view iOS applications, these project templates are not always suitable. In such cases, you can manually create segues between view controllers. When the user presses a particular control, the selected view controller will be presented. In this section, I'll show you how to manually create such a custom multi-view app of name *Navigation*. As Figure 4-11 shows, the app will have two view controllers: First View Controller and Second View Controller. Both of them will have associated views with labels describing a view controller. The user will be able to switch between views using *Switch view* or *Go back* buttons, depending on the currently displayed view.

Figure 4-11. *Views of the Navigation app, which we will develop in this section*

To implement the Navigation app, I use the Single View App project template, which targets iOS 9.0 and above. Then, I modify the view by adding a button and a label, configuring them as shown in the left part of Figure 4-11. Subsequently, I set the class of the initial view controller to FirstViewController, then add another view controller and set its class to SecondViewController. Then, I modify the view of the second view controller as shown in the right part of Figure 4-11. Lastly, I remove the ViewController.cs file, because it is not needed anymore.

Given the view controllers are ready, I define the first segue. As shown in Figure 4-12, I CTRL+Drag from the *Switch view* button to the second view controller. After releasing the left mouse button, a popup window appears. This popup allows me to choose the segue, which presents a new view controller. There are eight segue types to choose from. However, three of them (Non-Adaptive Action Segue group) are deprecated, and thus I do not discuss them. The other segues are the following:

- Show – displays the view of the selected view controller modally over the content of the current or source view controller. This segue can be also done programmatically with the ShowViewController method of the UIViewController.

- Show Detail – this segue corresponds to the UIViewController. ShowDetailViewController method and is only valid for the UISplitViewController. In this case, Show Detail replaces the second child view controller with the selected view controller. For other view controllers, Show Detail works like the Show segue.

- Present Modally – presents a view controller modally. Basically, it works similarly to the Show segue, but you can modify its presentation and transition styles.

- Popover Presentation – the effect of this segue depends on the actual size class. For screens with regular widths, the target view controller will appear as a popover, and modally (full-screen) on horizontally compact devices.

- Custom – custom-created segue. You can use this if none of the others are suitable.

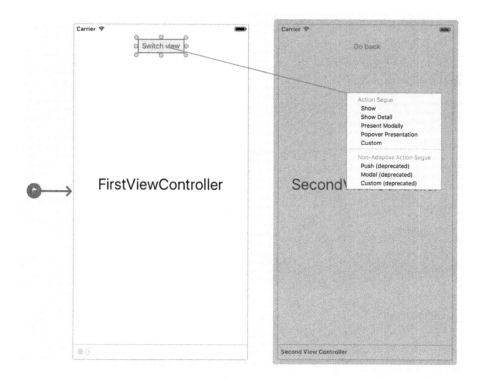

Figure 4-12. *Creating a segue between view controllers*

Here, I choose the Show segue, so after re-running the Navigation app, a view of the Second View Controller appears when you tap the *Switch view* button.

Editing a Segue

You can modify the segue by editing its properties. All created segues appear in the Document Outline pad. So far, we have only one segue, which appears under the `FirstViewController` item. As Figure 4-13 shows, you can use the properties of the segue to change its type (Show, Show Detail, Present Modally, or Popover Presentation). Depending on the segue type, additional controls appear. In my case, I change the segue type to Present Modally. Then, the Presentation and Transition drop-down lists appear. I use them to set the presentation and transition styles to Full Screen and Partial Curl, respectively.

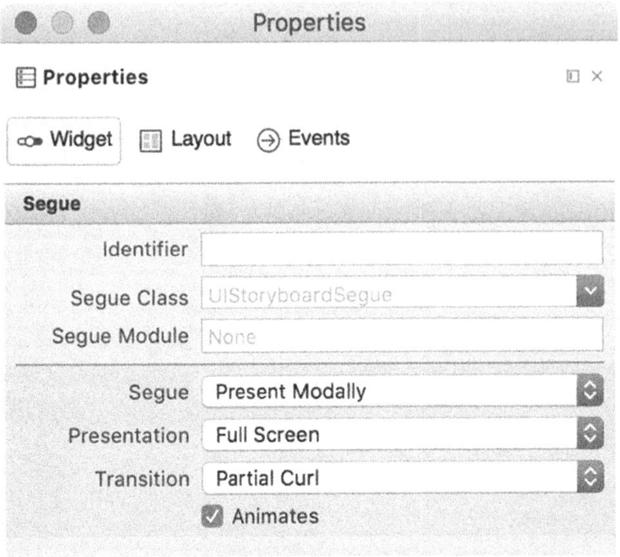

Figure 4-13. *Properties of the segue*

Unwind Segue

Although we created the segue, the user cannot go back to the First View Controller because the *Go back* button does not work yet. To enable such a feature, we need to create the Unwind segue, which is used to dismiss the view controller. To create such a segue, you first need to define the action so that the view controller will be unwound. This method is defined as the target of the Unwind segue.

To create the Unwind segue in the Navigation app, I supplement a definition of the FirstViewController class by the UnwindToFirstViewController method, which appears in Listing 4-12, and I also import a necessary namespace: System.Diagnostics. UnwindToFirstViewController is decorated with the Action attribute, so it can be invoked by the Objective-C runtime. Therefore, the iOS designer can recognize it, and we can now use this method for the Unwind segue.

Listing 4-12. An Action for the Unwind Segue

```
[Action("UnwindToFirstViewController:")]
public void UnwindToFirstViewController(UIStoryboardSegue segue)
{
    Debug.WriteLine("UnwindToFirstViewController");
}
```

To associate the UnwindToFirstViewController method with the *Go back* button, I open the visual designer and then CTRL+Drag from the *Go back* button to the green Exit icon, which is located on the bottom of the Second View Controller (Figure 4-14). After releasing the left mouse button, a popup window appears. This window contains a list of compatible action methods, which can be used for the segue. In my case, this list contains only one item, UnwindToFirstViewController. So, after choosing this item, I can re-run the app, and you will see that you can now navigate between the view controllers.

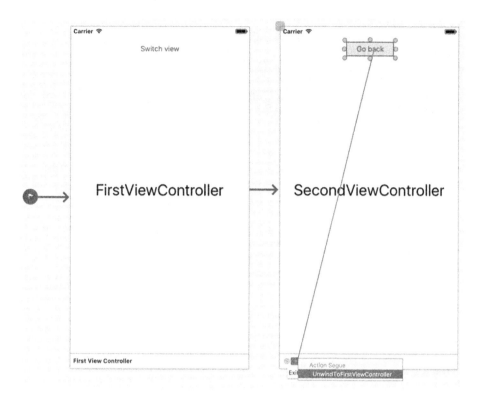

Figure 4-14. *Creating the unwind segue*

Preparing for Segues

Very often, you need to transfer data between view controllers. For instance, you show the view controller to collect user input, and after this view controller is dismissed, collected data is utilized in the initial view controller. To pass data between view controllers, you use the PrepareForSegue method of the UIViewController class. PrepareForSegue is invoked right before the segue is performed.

To present a sample usage of the PrepareForSegue class, I supplement the *Navigation* project with another class, BaseViewController, which I define according to Listing 4-13.

Listing 4-13. PrepareForSegue Method Outputs Names of Classes Implementing the Source and Destination View Controllers

```
public class BaseViewController : UIViewController
{
    protected BaseViewController(IntPtr handle) : base (handle){ }

    public override void PrepareForSegue(
        UIStoryboardSegue segue, NSObject sender)
    {
        base.PrepareForSegue(segue, sender);
```

```
        var sourceViewControllerName =
            segue.SourceViewController.GetType().Name;
        var destinationViewControllerName =
            segue.DestinationViewController.GetType().Name;

        Debug.WriteLine($"From: {sourceViewControllerName} " +
            $"To: {destinationViewControllerName}");
    }
}
```

The BaseViewController class derives from UIViewController, has a default constructor, and also overrides the PrepareForSegue method. Apart from the base functionality, PrepareForSegue reads the names of two classes, implementing the source and destination view controllers, and then displays them in the application output.

This example shows how to access instances of view controllers participating in the segue. Hence, to actually pass data between view controllers, you would need to supplement the associated classes with public properties and then rewrite them within the PrepareForSegue method.

To use the class from Listing 4-13, I modify declarations of the FirstViewController and the SecondViewController such that they derive from BaseViewController instead of UIViewController (as in Listing 4-3). So, when you re-run the app and perform navigation between the views, the output of the Navigation app should look like the one from Figure 4-15.

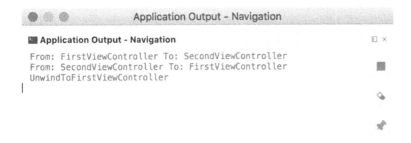

Figure 4-15. *Application output showing the flow of a segue*

Summary

In this chapter, we learned how to create multi-view applications and how to perform navigation between views using various approaches. We started with the Tabbed App project template and investigated how to create and modify tabs. Then, we moved to the Page-Based App project template. We deeply examined its relatively complex structure and then modified the app code to better understand page-based navigation. Finally, we created custom segues between view controllers. In the next chapter, we will learn how to handle touch gestures in iOS apps.

CHAPTER 5

Touch

Mobile devices are controlled by touch gestures. Users can use gestures to switch between views or to manipulate visual elements to translate, rotate, and resize them. In this chapter, we will learn how to handle gestures in Xamarin.iOS. We will start with a short description of gesture recognizers and then investigate how to use gestures for navigation. Subsequently, we will learn how to programmatically create and control gesture recognizers and the programmatic events they generate. Finally, we will implement the app, in which the location, rotation, and scale of the visual component will be controlled with gestures. So, after completing this chapter, you will know how to perform complex manipulation of visual controls, which you will find useful for media apps (like a photo editor or drawing tool) that extensively utilize gestures to tailor the appearance of visual elements.

Touches and Gesture Recognizers

Whenever the user touches the screen, a series of appropriate events are raised. To handle these events, you would normally need to implement the following methods in the class associated with the view controller:

- TouchesBegan, which is invoked when the user touches the screen with one or more fingers

- TouchesMoved, which is called when user changes the location of his or her fingers on the screen

- TouchesCancelled, which is invoked when the touch is canceled

- TouchesEnded, invoked when the touch gesture is finished

To show an actual sample, I create a new single view app (universal targeting iOS 9.0 and above) with the name *Touches*. Subsequently, I extend the definition of the ViewController class by the preceding methods and implement them according to Listing 5-1 (note that this code depends upon the following namespaces: Foundation, System.Diagnostics, and System.Linq). Implementation of TouchesBegan, TouchesCancelled, and TouchesEnded does not require any additional comments. All of these methods simply print the method name to the application output. A little more explanation is required for the TouchesMoved method. This function, apart from printing a *TouchesMoved* string, also iterates through the set of touches received by the event handler. In general, the application user can use more than one finger to perform a gesture. Each contact between his or her fingers and the screen is defined as a *touch*. The information about each touch is provided to the event handler as an instance of the NSSet. This object represents an unordered collection of objects, which in this specific case represents a touch. Hence, in Listing 5-1, the set of touches is first casted to a collection of UITouch objects, each of which is an abstract representation of the touch or finger movement on the screen. Then, I print the contact locations in the application output.

© Dawid Borycki 2018

D. Borycki, *Beginning Xamarin Development for the Mac*, https://doi.org/10.1007/978-1-4842-3132-6_5

Listing 5-1. Handling Low-level Information About Touches

```
public override void TouchesBegan(NSSet touches, UIEvent evt)
{
    base.TouchesBegan(touches, evt);

    Debug.WriteLine("TouchesBegan");
}

public override void TouchesMoved(NSSet touches, UIEvent evt)
{
    base.TouchesMoved(touches, evt);

    Debug.WriteLine("TouchesMoved");

    foreach (var touch in touches.Cast<UITouch>())
    {
        Debug.WriteLine(touch.GetPreciseLocation(View));
    }
}

public override void TouchesCancelled(NSSet touches, UIEvent evt)
{
    base.TouchesCancelled(touches, evt);

    Debug.WriteLine("TouchesCancelled");
}

public override void TouchesEnded(NSSet touches, UIEvent evt)
{
    base.TouchesEnded(touches, evt);

    Debug.WriteLine("TouchesEnded");
}
```

When you run the Touches app in the simulator, it will generate output that should look like that in Figure 5-1. As shown there, the beginning of the gesture is indicated by the TouchesBegan method. Subsequently, a series of TouchesMoved events is raised, each of which reports the current position of the touch contacts (where the finger touches the screen). Finally, TouchesEnded is fired, informing you that user has released his or her fingers from the screen.

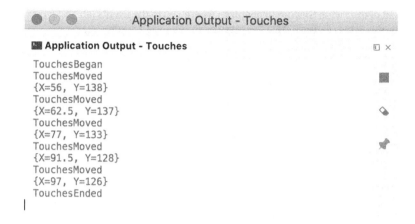

Figure 5-1. *A screenshot showing the sample output of the Touches app*

In order to recognize or detect a particular gesture, like swipe, long press, pan, rotation, or pinch, you would need to analyze the collection of touches to find patterns representing the particular gesture. More specifically, using the location of each contact, you would need to determine the touches' path. However, the iOS SDK provides several classes that do it for you. These classes are defined as *gesture recognizers* and greatly simplify gesture recognition because they implement all the necessary calculations. You only need to instantiate an appropriate gesture-recognizer class, and it will raise an appropriate event whenever it detects the particular gesture. As with most of the other iOS SDK components, gesture recognizers are wrapped by appropriate objects from Xamarin.iOS.

In the next few sections, I will tell you how to utilize gesture recognizers to perform navigation and to manipulate visual components.

Swipe and Long-Press Gesture Recognizers

To show how to use gesture recognizers, I extend the Navigation app we developed in the previous chapter so that the user will be able to switch between views using swipe and long-press gestures. Specifically, the long-press gesture will let him or her navigate from the first to the second view, while he or she will use the swipe gesture to navigate back to the first view. I will first create the swipe-gesture recognizer using the iOS designer, then generate a long-press gesture recognizer programmatically.

To implement such a functionality, I first copy the project folder under Chapter_05 of the companion code and then rename the project in Visual Studio (the Rename… option from the context menu) from *Navigation* to *Navigation.Swipe*. Subsequently, I open iOS designer, and from the Toolbox I drag Swipe Gesture Recognizer to the second view controller. A small icon representing this gesture recognizer appears at the bottom of the second view controller (see Figure 5-2).

Figure 5-2. *A Swipe Gesture Recognizer added to the view controller*

Then, I open the Properties pad of the Swipe Gesture Recognizer, where I go to the Events tab and type *SwipeDetected* into the Action drop-down list (Figure 5-3). After pressing Enter, Visual Studio creates an event handler, which I define according to Listing 5-2.

Figure 5-3. *Creating an event handler for the Swipe Gesture Recognizer*

Listing 5-2. Dismissing the View Controller When the Swipe Gesture Is Recognized

```
partial void SwipeDetected(UISwipeGestureRecognizer sender)
{
    DismissViewController(true, null);
}
```

When you re-run the app, you can navigate to the second view by tapping the *Switch view* button. Once the second view is displayed, you can go back to the first view by using the right-swipe gesture. Whenever such a gesture is detected, the recognizer raises an appropriate event, which is handled here by SwipeDetected. As Listing 5-2 shows, I use this method to navigate back using the DismissViewController method of the UIViewController class. DismissViewController accepts two arguments:

- animated – specifies if the transition between views should be animated
- completionHandler – lets you specify the code that is executed when the animation is completed

In Listing 5-2, I enable animation and pass null for the second argument of DismissViewController since I do not need to execute any additional methods.

Gesture recognizers also have several properties that let you adjust them to your specific needs. For instance, you can modify the swipe gesture recognizer to react to the selected swipe direction (see Figure 5-4). To this end, you use the Swipe drop-down list. Additionally, you can specify how many fingers are required for a swipe gesture (the Touches numeric control).

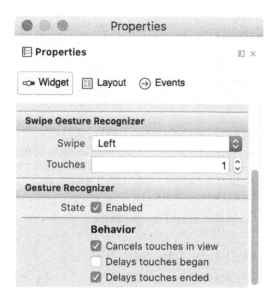

Figure 5-4. Properties of the swipe gesture recognizer

Let's now use the long-=press gesture recognizer to implement navigation from the first to the second view. To this end, I proceed as follows. First, I programmatically instantiate the UILongPressGestureRecognizer, a class representing the recognizer, in the ViewDidLoad method of the FirstViewController class (Listing 5-3). Then, I associate the resulting instance with the view using the AddGestureRecognizer method.

Listing 5-3. Programmatic Creation of the Gesture Recognizer

```
public override void ViewDidLoad()
{
    base.ViewDidLoad();

    var longPressGestureRecognizer =
        new UILongPressGestureRecognizer(PresentSecondViewController);

    View.AddGestureRecognizer(longPressGestureRecognizer);
}
```

As Listing 5-3 shows, the constructor of the UILongPressGestureRecognizer class accepts an argument pointing to an action, PresentSecondViewController, which is called whenever the gesture is recognized. In the previous case, we did the same thing (associate a method with the Action event) through the Properties pad. So now you know two equivalent methods of associating actions with gesture recognizers.

Listing 5-4. Presenting a View Controller

```
private void PresentSecondViewController(
    UILongPressGestureRecognizer sender)
{
    if(sender.State == UIGestureRecognizerState.Began)
    {
```

```
    var secondViewController = Storyboard.
        InstantiateViewController("SecondViewController")
        as UIViewController;

    PresentViewController(secondViewController, true, null);
  }
}
```

A definition of PresentSecondViewController appears in Listing 5-4. This method has a single argument, sender, which is of type UILongPressGestureRecognizer. This argument stores an instance of the gesture recognizer, which in this case detected the long-press gesture. In practice, you use this instance to get more information about the gesture. In particular, you can check the gesture state, which is represented by one of the following items from the UIGestureRecognizerState enumeration:

- Began – indicates that the gesture recognizer has identified a set of touches as the particular gesture

- Changed – specifies that touches (or finger positions) have been changed

- Possible – gesture recognizer has identified the set of touches but it is still processing them in order to recognize a gesture

- Ended, Cancelled, Failed – informs that the gesture has been completed, canceled, or failed (not recognized), respectively.

In Listing 5-4, I look for the Began state and then create the second view controller using the InstantiateViewController method of the Storyboard. Subsequently, I invoke PresentViewController to navigate to the second view controller. In order to instantiate the view controller using a Storyboard class, I need to set the storyboard identifier for the view controller. I do so using the Properties pad as shown in Figure 5-5.

If you now re-run the app, you can click and hold the mouse button in the first view. The second view will appear after a while. As you see, you can now navigate between the views using gestures and buttons.

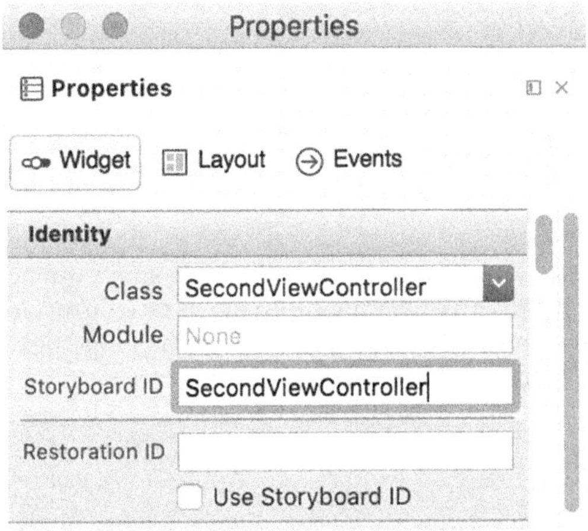

Figure 5-5. *Setting the storyboard identifier of the SecondViewController*

Manipulating Controls with Gestures

I will now tell you how to use gesture recognizers to manipulate controls. To this end, I will develop an app, shown in Figure 5-6. This app has a single control, an instance of the UIView class, which represents a purple square. This control will be translated with the pan gesture, rotated with the rotation gesture, and rescaled with the pinch gesture.

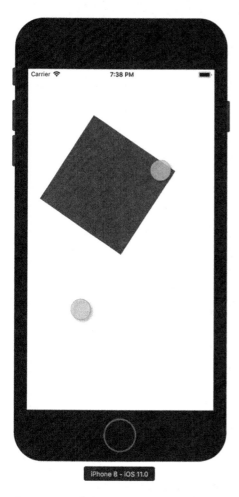

Figure 5-6. *The sample view of the Gestures app we will develop to learn about the pan, rotation and pinch gesture recognizers*

Pan Gesture Recognizer

I start by creating the *Gestures* app using the Single View App project template. I made this app universal and set the minimum target version to iOS 9.0. Then, in the ViewController class, I first import two namespaces: System.Drawing and CoreGraphics. Then, I declare one private field of type UIView. This field stores a reference to the purple rectangle. Afterward, I implement two private methods, AddSquare and AddPanGestureRecognizer (Listing 5-5).

Listing 5-5. Private Members of the ViewController Class

```
private UIView square;

private void AddSquare(float squareSideLength, UIColor color)
{
    square = new UIView()
    {
        BackgroundColor = color,
        Frame = new RectangleF(0, 0, squareSideLength, squareSideLength),
        Center = new CGPoint(View.Frame.Width / 2.0, View.Frame.Height / 2.0)
    };

    Add(square);
}

private void AddPanGestureRecognizer()
{
    var panGestureRecognizer =
        new UIPanGestureRecognizer(TranslateSquare);

    View.AddGestureRecognizer(panGestureRecognizer);
}
```

The AddSquare method is used to create and configure an instance of the UIView class, which represents the purple square. This method uses features that were already discussed, so further comments about AddSquare are not necessary. The second method from Listing 5-5, AddPanGestureRecognizer, first instantiates the UIPanGestureRecognizer and then associates it with the view. Whenever this object recognizes a pan gesture, it will invoke the TranslateSquare method from Listing 5-6.

Listing 5-6. Translating the Square

```
private void TranslateSquare(UIPanGestureRecognizer sender)
{
    var translation = sender.TranslationInView(View);

    square.Transform = CGAffineTransform.
        MakeTranslation(translation.X, translation.Y);
}
```

TranslateSquare reads the amount of translation made with the pan gesture using the TranslationInView method of the UIPanGestureRecognizer class instance. TranslationInView returns an instance of the CGPoint struct, whose X and Y properties store the relative translation along the horizontal and vertical directions, respectively. I then use those values to translate the square by modifying the Transform property of the UIView, to which a reference is contained in the square field. The Transform property is of type CGAffineTransform and represents the geometrical transformation of the particular visual component. In general, this transformation is called an *affine transform* and describes the translation, rotation, and scale changes of the visual control. For now, I only translate the square, so I create a translation transformation using the MakeTranslation static method of the CGAffineTransform struct. The MakeTranslation method accepts two arguments, which denote the amount of translation along the horizontal (first argument, tx) and vertical directions (second argument, ty). So, whenever the pan gesture is recognized, the square will be translated accordingly.

To actually use the AddSquare and AddPanGestureRecognizer methods, I modify the ViewDidLoad view event handler as shown in Listing 5-7. You can now run the Gestures app in the simulator and use the pan gesture—simply move the mouse cursor while holding the left mouse button. You will see that the square is translated as you move the mouse cursor within the view. However, you can easily notice that you can make the pan gesture anywhere in the view. Let's now modify the app such that it will only translate the square when the pan gesture is performed against it or, in other words, when you virtually hold the square. This requires detecting contact location, which is discussed in the next section.

Listing 5-7. ViewDidLoad Method of the ViewController

```
public override void ViewDidLoad()
{
    base.ViewDidLoad();

    AddSquare(50.0f, UIColor.Purple);

    AddPanGestureRecognizer();
}
```

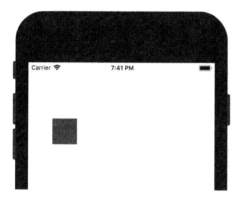

Figure 5-7. *Translating the square with the pan gesture*

Detecting Gesture Location

To get the location of the touch, you use the LocationInView method of the gesture-recognizer class instance. This method is available for all gesture recognizers because it is implemented in the UIGestureRecognizer class, which all other gesture recognizers derive from. You can also track the location of the particular touches (fingers) doing the gesture with the LocationOfTouch method. Both methods return the CGPoint struct. Its X and Y properties store the geometrical location of the gesture (or particular finger) on the screen.

In the Gestures app, I use the LocationInView method to check whether the pan gesture is performed on the purple square. As Listing 5-8 shows, I employ this method to implement another helper function, IsTouchLocationWithinSquare. The latter reads the touch location within the main view and then checks if it's contained within the square. To that end, I use the Contains method of the square.Frame property. Contains calculates if the X and Y components of the location (CGPoint struct) are within the rectangle (Frame property) enclosing the purple square. If so, I can translate the square. Therefore, I modify the TranslateSquare method (Listing 5-6) by first invoking IsTouchLocationWithinSquare. Then, if this method returns true, I create the translation transformation for the square (Listing 5-9).

Listing 5-8. A View Is Translated Only When the Pan Gesture Is Performed Over the Square

```
private bool IsTouchLocationWithinSquare(
    UIPanGestureRecognizer panGestureRecognizer)
{
    var location = panGestureRecognizer.LocationInView(View);

    return square.Frame.Contains(location.X, location.Y);
}
```

Listing 5-9. The Purple Square Is Translated Only When the Gesture Location Is Within the Bounds of This Control

```
private void TranslateSquare(UIPanGestureRecognizer sender)
{
    if (IsTouchLocationWithinSquare(sender))
    {
        var translation = sender.TranslationInView(View);

        square.Transform = CGAffineTransform.
            MakeTranslation(translation.X, translation.Y);
    }
}
```

If you now re-run the Gestures app, you will see that the square is translated only when you perform the pan gesture above this control. However, as you repeat this gesture, you will notice that a translation transformation of the purple square always has its origin at the center of the screen. This happens because the gesture recognizer calculates the shift made during a single gesture and does not take into account any translations made with previous gestures. To accurately translate the square, we would need to have the amount of the total translation accumulated during all gestures performed since the app was started. Therefore, we need to store the translation value after consecutive pan gestures have ended, and then add the resulting value to subsequent shifts. To implement such a functionality, I first supplement a definition of the ViewController with another private field, lastTranslation (of type CGPoint), and then modify the TranslateSquare method to store the amount of translation from when the gesture ended (Listing 5-10). To tally the amount of translation done during the single pan gesture, I read the x0 and y0 properties of the square.Transform property. I store the resulting values in the X and Y components of the lastTranslation member and add them to the actual translation transformation. Hence, when you re-run the app, the purple square "remembers" its position from the previous pan gesture. Therefore, all subsequent pan gestures correctly translate the purple square.

Listing 5-10. Accumulating the Translation of the Square

```
private CGPoint lastTranslation;

private void TranslateSquare(UIPanGestureRecognizer sender)
{
    if (IsTouchLocationWithinSquare(sender))
    {
        var translation = sender.TranslationInView(View);

        square.Transform = CGAffineTransform.MakeTranslation(
            translation.X + lastTranslation.X,
```

```
            translation.Y + lastTranslation.Y);
    }

    if (sender.State == UIGestureRecognizerState.Ended)
    {
        lastTranslation.X = square.Transform.x0;
        lastTranslation.Y = square.Transform.y0;
    }
}
```

Rotation and Pinch Gesture Recognizers

Let's now incorporate rotation and pinch gesture recognizers into the Gestures app so the purple square can be rotated and rescaled. The implementation of this sample requires several components. I will start with a method that combines a translation, rotation, and scaling into a single affine transformation. Then, I will tell you how to programmatically create the rotation and pinch gesture recognizers and enable simultaneous gesture recognition.

A Total Affine Transformation

Mathematically, the affine transformation can be represented as the 3×3 transformation matrix, T:

$$T = \begin{bmatrix} xx & xy & 0 \\ yx & yy & 0 \\ x0 & y0 & 1 \end{bmatrix}$$

Each element of this matrix from the first and second columns corresponds to the appropriate fields of the CGAffineTransform struct. So, in general, you can implement the total affine transformation by manually calculating values for matrix elements. For instance, if you want to translate an object, you write shift values along the horizontal and vertical directions to the x0 and y0 properties, respectively. Scaling and rotation require a little bit more mathematics:

$$xx = sx \times cos(\alpha),$$

$$xy = sin(\alpha),$$

$$yx = -sin(\alpha),$$

$$yy = sy \times cos(\alpha),$$

where sx and sy denote the scaling factors along the horizontal and vertical directions, while α is the rotation angle.

Hopefully, the CGAffineTransform delivers methods that simplify these calculations. More specifically, to create the total affine transformation, I combine the following static methods of the CGAffineTransform struct:

- MakeIdentity, which creates the identity transformation. It's a special form of the affine transformation that does not modify the visual control. MakeIdentity sets the xx, xy, yx, and yy properties of the CGAffineTransform to ones, and x0, y0 to zeros.

- Translate, which updates the x0 and y0 properties of CGAffineTransform

- Rotate, which updates xx, xy, yx, and yy elements of the transformation matrix without changing the scaling factors

- Scale, which changes the scaling factors (sx and sy) and includes them in the following properties of CGAffineTransform: xx, xy, yx, and yy, but without changing the rotation angle

I utilize the preceding methods in the UpdateSquareTransform method in Listing 5-11. This method also includes the previous translation, rotation, and scale values. To this end, values stored in the lastTranslation and lastRotation fields are added to the current translation and rotation, while the current scale factor is multiplied by the previous one. This is because the scaling operation is multiplicative, while shifts and rotations are additive (see preceding equations).

Listing 5-11. Implementation of the Total Affine Transformation for the Purple Square

```
private nfloat lastRotation;
private nfloat lastScale = 1.0f;

private void UpdateSquareTransform(CGPoint translation,
    nfloat rotation, nfloat scale)
{
    var transform = CGAffineTransform.MakeIdentity();

    // Include previous translation, rotation, and scale
    translation.X += lastTranslation.X;
    translation.Y += lastTranslation.Y;
    rotation += lastRotation;
    scale *= lastScale;

    // Combine translation, rotation, and scale
    transform = CGAffineTransform.Translate(
        transform, translation.X, translation.Y);
    transform = CGAffineTransform.Rotate(transform, rotation);
    transform = CGAffineTransform.Scale(transform, scale, scale);

    square.Transform = transform;
}
```

Given the UpdateSquareTransform method, I first modify the TranslateSquare function as shown in Listing 5-12 and then implement two other methods (Listing 5-13), which be used later by the rotation and pinch gesture recognizers.

Listing 5-12. An Updated Definition of the TranslateSquare Method

```
private void TranslateSquare(UIPanGestureRecognizer sender)
{
    if (IsTouchLocationWithinSquare(sender))
    {
        var translation = sender.TranslationInView(View);

        //square.Transform = CGAffineTransform.MakeTranslation(
        //    translation.X + lastTranslation.X,
        //    translation.Y + lastTranslation.Y);

        UpdateSquareTransform(translation, 0.0f, 1.0f);
    }

    if (sender.State == UIGestureRecognizerState.Ended)
    {
        lastTranslation.X = square.Transform.x0;
        lastTranslation.Y = square.Transform.y0;
    }
}
```

Listing 5-13. Rotating and Scaling the Purple Square (note that scaling factors are equal along horizontal and vertical directions)

```
private void RotateSquare(UIRotationGestureRecognizer sender)
{
    UpdateSquareTransform(new CGPoint(), sender.Rotation, 1.0f);

    if (sender.State == UIGestureRecognizerState.Ended)
    {
        lastRotation += sender.Rotation;
    }
}

private void ScaleSquare(UIPinchGestureRecognizer sender)
{
    UpdateSquareTransform(new CGPoint(), 0.0f, sender.Scale);

    if (sender.State == UIGestureRecognizerState.Ended)
    {
        lastScale *= sender.Scale;
    }
}
```

Rotating and Scaling the Control

Finally, all I need to do is create two additional gesture recognizers—one for rotation and the second for a pinch. To do so, in the ViewController class I implement the AddRotationAndPinchGestureRecognizers method (Listing 5-14) and then invoke it in the ViewDidLoad event handler (Listing 5-15).

Listing 5-14. Creating Rotation and Pinch Gesture Recognizers

```
private void AddRotationAndPinchGestureRecognizers()
{
    var rotationGestureRecognizer =
        new UIRotationGestureRecognizer(RotateSquare);
    var pinchGestureRecognizer =
        new UIPinchGestureRecognizer(ScaleSquare);

    View.AddGestureRecognizer(pinchGestureRecognizer);
    View.AddGestureRecognizer(rotationGestureRecognizer);
}
```

Listing 5-15. Adding the Support for Rotation and Pinch Gestures

```
public override void ViewDidLoad()
{
    base.ViewDidLoad();

    AddSquare(50.0f, UIColor.Purple);

    AddPanGestureRecognizer();

    AddRotationAndPinchGestureRecognizers();
}
```

After re-running the app, you will see results similar to Figure 5-6. Note that to perform rotation and pinch gestures you need to use multi-touch, which you enable in the simulator using the ALT key. It activates two rectangles, representing two fingers. Then, you press the left mouse button and either rotate fingers (rotation gesture) or change the distance between them (pinch gesture). You will note that the purple square is transformed according to your virtual touches. However, only one gesture recognizer runs at a time, which means, for instance, that you cannot perform a pinch gesture while rotating the square. This is because such simultaneous gesture recognition is disabled by default. I'll tell you how to enable it next.

Simultaneous Gesture Recognition

To enable simultaneous gesture recognition, you use the ShouldRecognizeSimultaneously property of the gesture-recognizer class. Listing 5-16 shows how to enable simultaneous gesture recognition for the rotate and pinch gestures.

Listing 5-16. Enabling Simultaneous Gesture Recognition

```
private UIRotationGestureRecognizer rotationGestureRecognizer;
private UIPinchGestureRecognizer pinchGestureRecognizer;

private void AddRotationAndPinchGestureRecognizers()
{
    rotationGestureRecognizer =
        new UIRotationGestureRecognizer(RotateSquare);
    pinchGestureRecognizer =
        new UIPinchGestureRecognizer(ScaleSquare);
```

```
    rotationGestureRecognizer.ShouldRecognizeSimultaneously
        += GestureRecognizer_ShouldRecognizeSimultaneously;
    pinchGestureRecognizer.ShouldRecognizeSimultaneously
        += GestureRecognizer_ShouldRecognizeSimultaneously;

    View.AddGestureRecognizer(pinchGestureRecognizer);
    View.AddGestureRecognizer(rotationGestureRecognizer);
}

private bool GestureRecognizer_ShouldRecognizeSimultaneously(
    UIGestureRecognizer RgestureRecognizer,
    UIGestureRecognizer otherGestureRecognizer)
{
    return true;
}
```

Rotation and pinch gestures can now be processed simultaneously. Therefore, you also need to update the RotateSquare and ScaleSquare methods to include the fact that a square can be rescaled when rotated. For this reason, in Listing 5-16, references to both gesture recognizers were stored in the fields of the ViewController class. Then, you use this reference to update the rotation and scale changes of the square, as shown in Listing 5-17.

Listing 5-17. Scale Changes Are Included During Rotation

```
private void RotateSquare(UIRotationGestureRecognizer sender)
{
    //UpdateSquareTransform(new CGPoint(), sender.Rotation, 1.0f);

    if (sender.State == UIGestureRecognizerState.Changed)
    {
        if (pinchGestureRecognizer.State == UIGestureRecognizerState.Changed)
        {
            UpdateSquareTransform(new CGPoint(),
                sender.Rotation, pinchGestureRecognizer.Scale);
        }
        else
        {
            UpdateSquareTransform(new CGPoint(), sender.Rotation, 1.0f);
        }
    }

    if (sender.State == UIGestureRecognizerState.Ended)
    {
        lastRotation += sender.Rotation;
    }
}
```

```
private void ScaleSquare(UIPinchGestureRecognizer sender)
{
    // UpdateSquareTransform(new CGPoint(), 0.0f, sender.Scale);

    if (sender.State == UIGestureRecognizerState.Changed)
    {
        if (rotationGestureRecognizer.State == UIGestureRecognizerState.Changed)
        {
            UpdateSquareTransform(new CGPoint(),
                rotationGestureRecognizer.Rotation, sender.Scale);
        }
        else
        {
            UpdateSquareTransform(new CGPoint(), 0.0f, sender.Scale);
        }
    }
    if (sender.State == UIGestureRecognizerState.Ended)
    {
        lastScale *= sender.Scale;
    }
}
```

Both methods from Listing 5-17 work similarly, so I will only discuss the first one, RotateSquare. In this method, I first check if the rotation gesture has been correctly recognized. To this end, I read the State property of the UIRotationGestureRecognizer class instance provided by the sender argument. Subsequently, I invoke UpdateSquareTransform. The parameters of this method depend on whether the user does the pinch gesture in parallel with the rotation. If so, I pass the scale changes obtained from the pinch gesture recognizer as the last parameter of the UpdateSquareTransform. However, if the user does not re-scale the purple square during rotation, I simply pass 1 for this last parameter. It indicates that the scale should not be changed. Lastly, I store the accumulated rotation in the lastRotation member.

I encourage you to independently extend the Gestures app such that it will simultaneously recognize not only rotation and pinch gestures but also the pan gesture.

Summary

In this chapter, we created three sample apps, which show you how to work with touch in Xamarin.iOS. You learned how to employ gestures to implement navigation between views and also how to manipulate visual controls with various gesture recognizers. Along the way, you learned about the gesture states, simultaneous gesture recognition, and the CGAffineTransform struct, which helps you to arbitrarily transform objects with the affine transformation.

CHAPTER 6

Unit Testing

Achieving high-quality apps is one of the most important and difficult tasks in software engineering, especially in mobile development. Mobile apps usually have a lot of competing solutions, and therefore to make your app successful you need to ensure that the app works correctly on various mobile devices. This requires you to repeat the same testing for your app on many devices, which can be a very long and expensive process. Unit, or automatic, testing is therefore not only another fancy tool for developers but also becomes a habit in software engineering. Automatic tests can be run right after code compilation as many times as needed to ensure that new features do not affect other project components. As a result, you can easily track app development and its maintenance. Automatic testing is not limited to validating the functionality of the logic layer but can also be utilized to test the user interface. More specifically, automatic UI tests synthesize user actions to interact with the visual components (or views) of the app exactly the same as a human would.

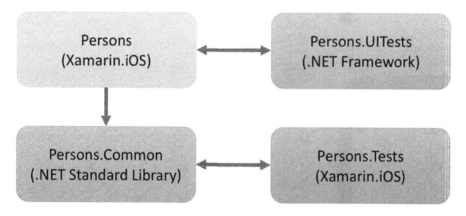

Figure 6-1. *A diagram showing the relationships between the projects we will implement in this chapter. Single arrows represent references only, while double arrows indicate projects that will be tested automatically.*

In this chapter, I will show you how to implement automatic unit and UI tests. To this end, I will create several projects that will be related to each other as shown in Figure 6-1. Clearly, I will have a single view iOS app, *Persons*. This app targets the Xamarin.iOS framework and uses a model class, Person. The Person class will be implemented in a separate, reusable .NET Standard Library project, *Persons.Common*. The Persons app has the UI shown in Figure 6-2. There is one button, four labels, and four text fields. When you tap the button, a default person's data (first and last name, email, and age) will be displayed in the text fields.

To validate this functionality, I will have two test projects: *Persons.Tests* and *Persons.UITests*. The first one, Persons.Tests, will be a standard Xamarin.iOS app that implements the test runner shown in Figure 6-3. This project will be used to test the Person class. In particular, I will check the public property setters and public

© Dawid Borycki 2018
D. Borycki, *Beginning Xamarin Development for the Mac*, https://doi.org/10.1007/978-1-4842-3132-6_6

methods. The second test project, Persons.UITests, is a .NET Framework Class Library and will be invoked by the Xamarin UI Test Framework to validate the UI of the Persons app. In particular, I will implement a test that will virtually tap a button and then check whether the text fields possess the expected values. Finally, I will show how to run the UI tests in the Xamarin Test Cloud (XTC). XTC provides you with cloud-based access to a farm of physical devices with various screens and operating systems. Therefore, you can automatically test your app to ensure it will be compatible with all target devices. XTC has a web-based interface that even lets you visualize how your app will look on the devices on which you choose to run your UI tests (Figure 6-4).

Figure 6-2. *User interface of the Persons app*

Figure 6-3. *Unit test runner*

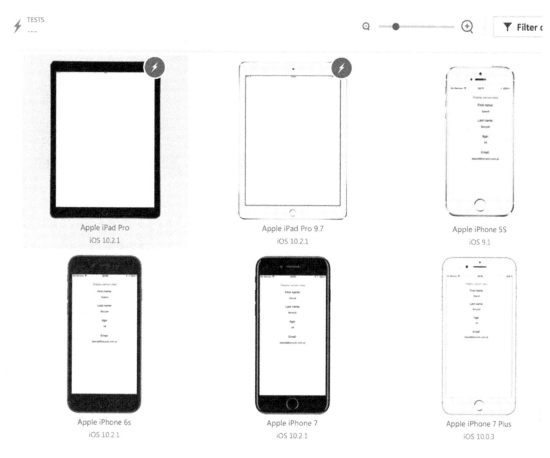

Figure 6-4. *An example report showing results of UI tests executed on a number of physical devices from the Xamarin Test Cloud*

Creating a Model to Test

I start by implementing a Persons.Common shared library, which I create with the .NET Standard Library project template (Figure 6-5). Within this project, I make a new folder, Models, in which I save a Person.cs file with a definition of the Person class given in Listing 6-1. This class has four public properties, three of which are of type string. They store first and last name and an email address. The last property, Age, is of the integral (int) type and is used to store the age of the given person. Additionally, a Person class defines two public methods. The first, FullName, returns a first and last name combined into one string. The second method, IsEmailValid, implements a very simple verification of the email address. This method only checks whether the given string contains the @ symbol. Of course, this algorithm is too primitive to effectively validate an email address. However, it will be the goal of one of our unit tests to find this issue.

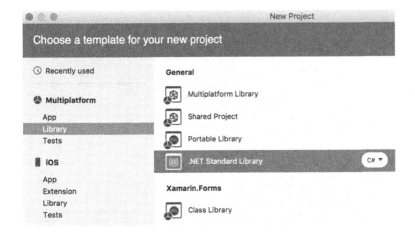

Figure 6-5. *Creating a shared library*

Listing 6-1. A Definition of the Model to Be Tested

```
public class Person
{
    public string FirstName { get; set; }

    public string LastName { get; set; }

    public string Email { get; set; }

    public int Age { get; set; }

    public string FullName()

    {
        return $"{FirstName} {LastName}";
    }

    public static bool IsEmailValid(string email)
    {
        return email.Contains("@");
    }
}
```

Implementing Unit Tests

Given the model to test, we can implement actual unit tests that verify its functionality. To that end, I create another project named *Persons.Tests* using a Unit Test App project template. The location of this template in the New Project dialog is shown in Figure 6-6. Then, I configure the unit test app in the same way as I would any other iOS app (see Figure 6-7). More specifically, I make this app universal so it is compatible with iPhones and iPads, and then I set the target version to iOS 9.0. Finally, I choose a location for my project and create it.

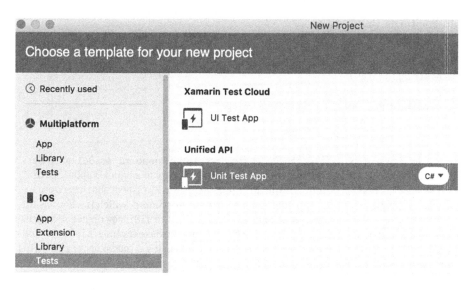

Figure 6-6. *Creating the unit test app project*

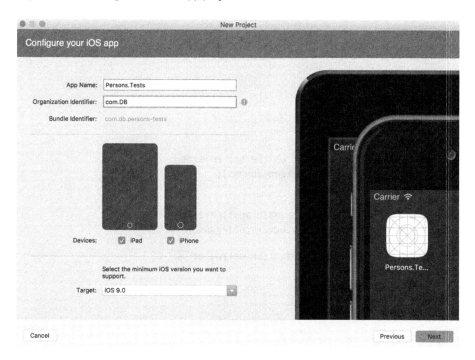

Figure 6-7. *Configuring Persons.Tests unit test app*

After creating the unit test app, you will see that its structure is the same as that of a typical iOS app. In particular, as Listing 6-2 shows, this app has a standard Main method that starts the UI of the app with the UnitTestAppDelegate class.

Listing 6-2. The Entry Point of the Unit Test App

```
public class Application
{
    static void Main(string[] args)
    {
        UIApplication.Main(args, null, "UnitTestAppDelegate");
    }
}
```

Listing 6-3 features a definition of the UnitTestAppDelegate class. As the "standard" AppDelegate class, UnitTestAppDelegate derives from UIApplicationDelegate. However, contrary to a typical AppDelegate like those we have used so far, UnitTestAppDelegate explicitly implements the FinishedLaunching app event handler. This is because the Persons.Tests app does not have a main storyboard, which is what sets the initial view controller. Instead, this is done programmatically by instantiating the UIWindow object, setting its RootViewController property, and making the window visible by invoking the MakeKeyAndVisible method of the UIWindow class instance. We see that the root view controller is created using a TouchRunner class. This class is provided by the NUnit testing framework and provides the UI, which is then used to execute the unit tests (refer back to Figure 6-3).

Listing 6-3. A Full Definition of the UnitTestAppDelegate

```
[Register("UnitTestAppDelegate")]
public partial class UnitTestAppDelegate : UIApplicationDelegate
{
    UIWindow window;
    TouchRunner runner;

    public override bool FinishedLaunching(
        UIApplication app, NSDictionary options)
    {
        // create a new window instance based on the screen size
        window = new UIWindow(UIScreen.MainScreen.Bounds);
        runner = new TouchRunner(window);

        // register every test included in the main application/assembly
        runner.Add(System.Reflection.Assembly.GetExecutingAssembly());

        window.RootViewController = new UINavigationController(
            runner.GetViewController());

        // make the window visible
        window.MakeKeyAndVisible();

        return true;
    }
}
```

Before we can test the model, we need to configure references. Note that the Person class is defined in a separate project with respect to Persons.Tests, so the latter has to reference the Persons.Common library. To configure this reference, you use the Reference Manager (Figure 6-8). To open this window, you go to Solution Explorer, navigate to the Persons.Tests project, and then use the "Edit References..." option from the context menu of the References node. Once in Reference Manager, you go to the Projects tab and select the Persons.Common project as shown in Figure 6-8. The Person class can now be used inside Persons.Tests.

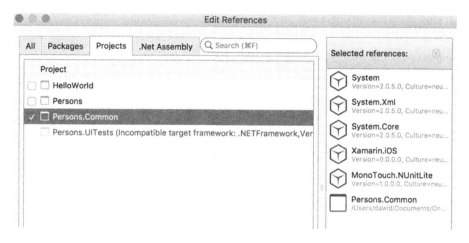

Figure 6-8. *Reference Manager showing the Persons.Tests project*

To implement the actual unit tests, I supplement the Persons.Tests project with a new file, `PersonTests.cs`. To create this file, I use the New File dialog, in which I select the "Unit tests" object from the iOS tab (Figure 6-9). The default content of the `PersonTests.cs` file shows how to create the test class and test methods that actually perform unit testing. More specifically, the test class has to be decorated by the `TestFixtureAttribute` (see Listing 6-4). This attribute instructs the testing framework to look for test methods in this class. Note that the `PersonTests` class is public. Otherwise, the NUnit testing framework would not recognize it.

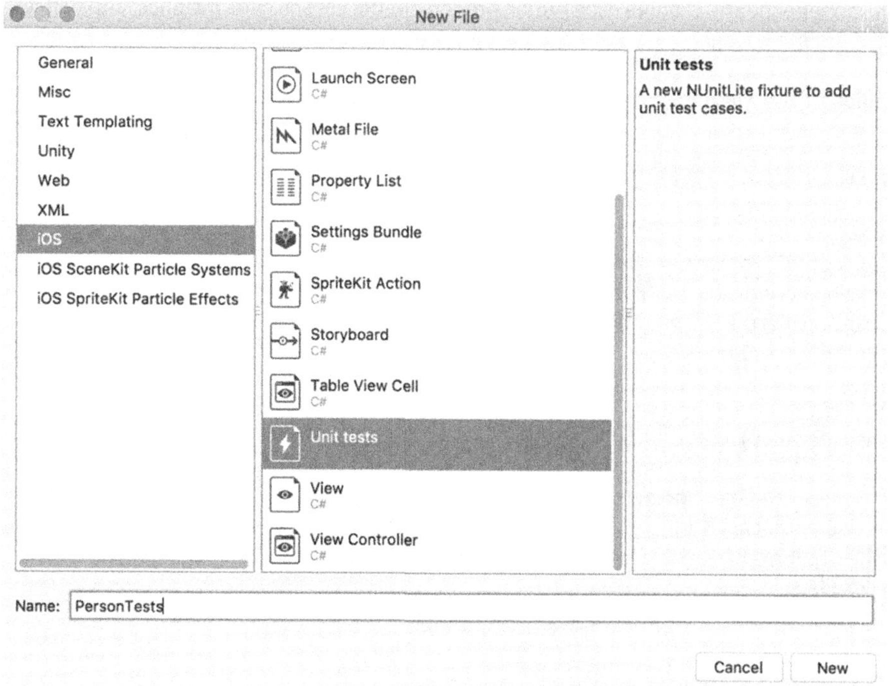

Figure 6-9. *Adding the unit tests file*

Listing 6-4. A Declaration of the PersonTests Class

```
[TestFixture]
public class PersonTests
```

The default tests given in the PersonTests.cs file do not implement anything useful, but they do show how to define a test method. Namely, such a method has to be a public function of the test class. Moreover, a test method does not return any value and is decorated with a TestAttribute. Every method that conforms to these requirements will be seen by the TouchRunner and displayed in its UI.

To define the actual tests, I first import two additional namespaces, Persons.Common.Models and System.Text.RegularExpressions, and then replace the default definition of the PersonTests class with three test methods: VerifyPublicProperties, VerifyFullName, and VerifyEmail. The first one, VerifyPublicProperties, appears in Listing 6-5. The general structure of this and any other test method comprises three well-separated blocks of code: arrange, act, and assert. In the following listings, each of these blocks is marked by an appropriate comment. In the arrange block, you typically prepare the input data for your test. Therefore, in Listing 6-5, I declare four constants, which are then used in the act block to invoke the logic being tested. Here, I validate public property setters of the Person class. So, I instantiate this class with a default constructor and then set the values of its public properties to previously declared constants. Then, in the assert block, I verify if, indeed, public properties of the Person class instance possess the expected values.

To validate values being tested, you use static methods of the NUnit.Framework.Assert class. If you have previously worked with Visual Studio for Windows, you probably already know the Assert class from the Microsoft.VisualStudio.TestPlatform.UnitTestFramework package. Both classes work similarly and expose analogous functionality. In particular, the AreEqual method I use in Listing 6-5 compares two variables and raises an exception of type NUnit.Framework.AssertionException whenever the values of these variables differ. Additionally, you can define the message that is displayed when this assertion is raised. In Listing 6-5, I independently validate each public property of the Person class instance, and hence each assertion has a different message.

Listing 6-5. A Definition of Test Method, Which Validates Public Property Setters

```
[Test]
public void VerifyPublicProperties()
{
    // Arrange
    const string expectedFirstName = "Dawid";
    const string expectedLastName = "Borycki";
    const string expectedEmail = "dawid@borycki.com.pl";
    const int expectedAge = 34;

    // Act
    var person = new Person()
    {
        FirstName = expectedFirstName,
        LastName = expectedLastName,
        Email = expectedEmail,
        Age = expectedAge
    };

    // Assert
    Assert.AreEqual(expectedFirstName, person.FirstName,
        "Incorrect first name");
```

```
    Assert.AreEqual(expectedLastName, person.LastName,
        "Incorrect last name");
    Assert.AreEqual(expectedEmail, person.Email,
        "Incorrect e-mail");
    Assert.AreEqual(expectedAge, person.Age,
        "Incorrect age");
}
```

The second test method, VerifyFullName, validates a FullName method of the Person class instance. Basically, VerifyFullName works in a way similar to VerifyPublicProperties. Namely, in the VerifyFullName method, I first declare the expected values within the arrange block. Then, I use these values to instantiate a Person class (act block). Finally, I invoke the FullName method and check if its result is the same as the expected one.

You may wonder why I implement such relatively simple test methods when I know a definition of the Person class. Typically, as a unit tester, you do not have such a privilege. Instead, you have to write test methods that fully cover a class definition, but you typically do not have access to the source code. So, in general, you start with simple test methods, validate basic class functionality, and then increase the complexity of your tests. By doing so, you ensure that the class is properly tested from the ground up.

Such an approach is also utilized in test-driven development (TDD). In TDD, you first implement the class skeleton, and then write appropriate unit tests. At this first stage, all tests should fail due to the lack of actual class implementations. Subsequently, you start implementing a class, and iteratively run unit tests to ensure that your implementation is valid. You continue this process as long as all tests have been passed. TDD is also beneficial when you modify and extend your app. You run unit tests after introducing any change to your code to ensure that it does not affect a functionality that is already implemented.

Listing 6-6. Validating a FullName Method of the Person Class Instance

```
[Test]
public void VerifyFullName()
{
    // Arrange
    const string expectedFirstName = "Dawid";
    const string expectedLastName = "Borycki";

    string expectedFullName = $"{expectedFirstName} {expectedLastName}";

    // Act
    var person = new Person()
    {
        FirstName = expectedFirstName,
        LastName = expectedLastName
    };

    // Assert
    Assert.AreEqual(expectedFullName, person.FullName());
}
```

The last test method of the PersonTests class, VerifyEmail, appears in Listing 6-7. This method aims at validating the IsEmailValid static method of the Person class. Following what I said before, VerifyEmail has a more complex implementation. More specifically, in the arrange block, I start by declaring an email to be checked. In this example, this email is invalid because it does not contain a domain. Then, in the act block, I perform the validation of the email string using a regular expression. This is implemented in a private helper method, PersonsTests.EmailCheck. Since this method does not conform to test-method requirements, it will not be recognized by the test runner.

The EmailCheck function utilizes the Regex class from the .NET Framework. This class is used to perform operations with regular expressions. In particular, I use the IsMatch static method to check whether a regular expression pattern matches the given string. The pattern I use in Listing 6-7 matches every string that contains a combination of letters and digits followed by the @ sign and a domain name. The result of this match is then compared to the value returned by the Person.IsEmailValid method. Because the latter uses a very naive way of validating an email address, this test should fail. To see that, we need to run the test methods we implemented.

Listing 6-7. Validating Email Address

```
[Test]
public void VerifyEmail()
{
    // Arrange
    const string email = "dawid@";

    // Act
    var isValid = EmailCheck(email);

    // Assert
    Assert.AreEqual(isValid, Person.IsEmailValid(email));
}

private bool EmailCheck(string email)
{
    const string emailPattern = "[A-Z0-9a-z._%+-]+@[A-Za-z0-9.-]+\\.[A-Za-z]{2,}";

    return Regex.IsMatch(email, emailPattern);
}
```

Running Unit Tests

To run the unit tests, you set the Persons.Tests app as a startup project. To do so, use the Solution Explorer, where you right-click the Persons.Tests node and then choose the "Set As Startup Project" option from the context menu (Figure 6-10). You then run the app by using the Run menu or by pressing a *Play* button in the Debug Target pad. After a while, the Persons.Tests app or test runner will be launched in the simulator and will look analogous to Figure 6-11.

Build Persons.Tests   ⌘K
Rebuild Persons.Tests   ^⌘K
Clean Persons.Tests   ⇧⌘K
Unload

Archive for Publishing
View Archives

Run Item
Start Debugging Item
Run With   ▶
Set As Startup Project

Add   ▶

Figure 6-10. *Setting Persons.Tests as startup project*

The test runner will display any information about the test methods it recognized. Now, you can run all these unit tests by clicking the *Run Everything* button, or you can select Persons.Tests.exe and then PersonsTests. A list of test methods appears, as shown earlier in Figure 6-3. You can run each test individually by pressing a corresponding entry or run them all by clicking the *Run all* button. After a short while, the results of each test method will be displayed. We see that only one test method (VerifyEmail) fails.

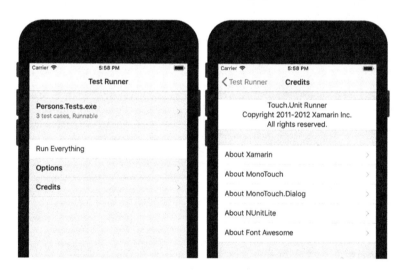

Figure 6-11. *A test runner*

User Interface Tests

After validating the Person class, we can move forward and use it to implement the Persons app. Subsequently, we will test its UI with the Xamarin UI Tests framework and Xamarin Test Cloud (XTC).

Creating an App

I create the Persons app with a Single View iOS app template (which supports iOS 9.0 and later). Subsequently, I define the UI of this app as shown earlier in Figure 6-2. Namely, I create one button, four labels, and four text fields. I now set the name and accessibility identifier (Figure 6-12) of each text field to `TextFieldFirstName`, `TextFieldLastName`, `TextFieldEmail`, and `TextFieldAge`, respectively. Names will be used to set the text properties of each `TextField` in C# code, while accessibility identifiers will be used to find controls in the UI test. Subsequently, I double-click the button to create the `TouchUpInside` event handler, and for now I leave this method empty. Finally, I edit the references such that the Persons app references the Person.Common library.

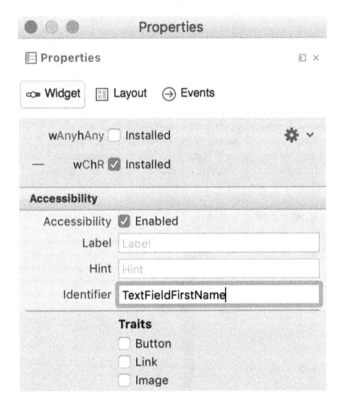

Figure 6-12. *Configuring accessibility identifier*

Xamarin Test Cloud Agent

To enable a test runner to interact with the Persons app, you use the Xamarin Test Cloud Agent, which you install as a NuGet package. To install it, you can either go to Solution Explorer and then select the "Add Packages..." option from the context menu of the Persons/Packages node or use menu Project ➤ Add NuGet Packages.... Regardless of the method you choose, the Add Packages dialog appears. In this dialog, you go to the search box and type *Xamarin Test Cloud Agent*. A list of matched packages appears on the left, as shown in Figure 6-13. You then choose the first element on the list and click the *Add Package* button.

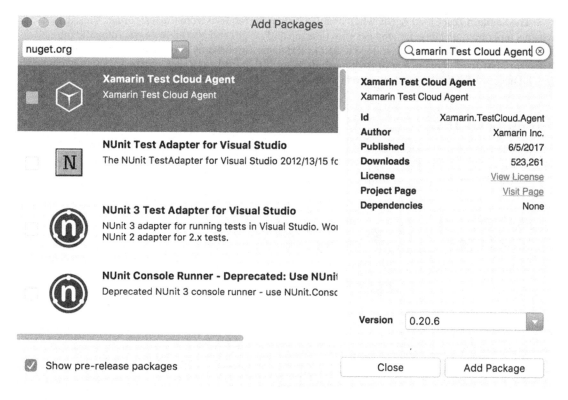

Figure 6-13. *Installing the Xamarin Test Cloud Agent NuGet package*

After a short while, the NuGet package will be added to the Persons project. Then, you just need to enable it by adding the following statement (Listing 6-8), `Xamarin.Calabash.Start()`, to the `FinishedLaunching` event handler. This event handler is defined in the `AppDelegate.cs` file of the Persons project. Since the app cannot be submitted to the store with the Xamarin Test Cloud Agent enabled, a corresponding statement from Listing 6-8 is surrounded by the C# preprocessor directives and is executed only when the `ENABLE_TEST_CLOUD` symbol is defined. This is done by default in the Debug configuration of the tested app after installing a Xamarin Test Cloud Agent NuGet package. To see this, go to the options of the Persons project and then open the Build/Compiler tab. `ENABLE_TEST_CLOUD` will be listed within the Define Symbols text box. If you change the configuration to *Release*, this symbol is undefined.

Listing 6-8. Setting Up the Xamarin Test Cloud Agent

```
public override bool FinishedLaunching(
    UIApplication application, NSDictionary launchOptions)
{
#if ENABLE_TEST_CLOUD
    Xamarin.Calabash.Start();
#endif

    return true;
}
```

The Xamarin Test Cloud Agent, when enabled, listens for requests from the test runner. This agent accepts programmatically generated gestures (like tap and swipe) and also allows a test runner to interact with visual controls; for example, to read text from text fields. Importantly, the test runner can also use the Xamarin Test Cloud Agent to take app screenshots to verify that the layout is correct on various devices and that all necessary controls are visible and in expected locations when the device is rotated.

Creating UI Tests

To create the test runner, which will send requests to Xamarin Test Cloud Agent to test the UI of the Persons app, I add the new project, Persons.UITests, which I make using the UI Test App project template in Visual Studio (Figure 6-14).

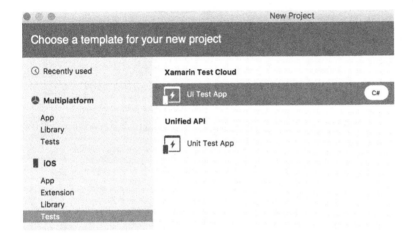

Figure 6-14. *UI Test App project template in the New Project dialog*

After creating Persons.UITests, we can note that this project, unlike Persons.Tests, does not have the typical structure of an iOS app. Moreover, by comparing both projects, we see that they target different frameworks and compile to different targets. To see this, go to Solution Explorer and select "Options" from the context menu of each project, then go to the Build/General tab ➤ Target framework and compile the target shown on top (see Figure 6-15).

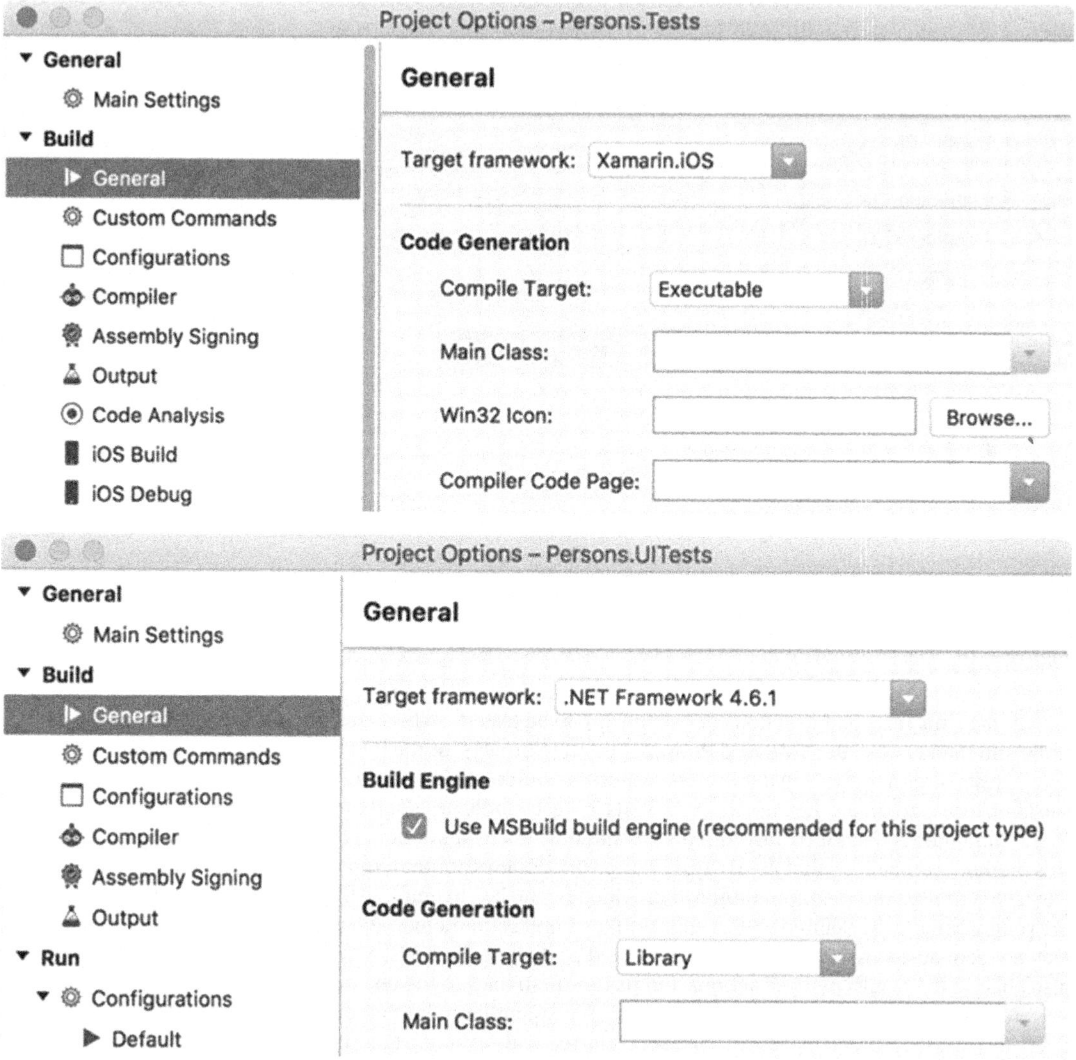

Figure 6-15. *General options of the build options of the Persons.Tests (top) and Persons.UITests projects*

As Figure 6-15 shows, Persons.Tests is the Xamarin.iOS executable app and runs directly on the device or a simulator as with any other iOS app. In this case, you invoke test methods using the UI of the test runner (refer back to Figure 6-3). On the other side of things, Persons.UITests is the .NET Framework Class Library. Since it is not compiled to the executable, it is run indirectly. Every test method implemented within Persons.UITests is invoked by the Xamarin.UITest framework. To associate the apps that will be executed by this framework using the Unit Tests pad, you go to View ➤ Pads ➤ Unit Tests. A window as shown in Figure 6-16 appears.

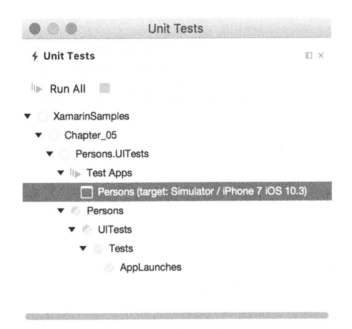

Figure 6-16. *The Unit Tests pad*

In the Unit Tests pad, you first choose the app to be tested. To that end, you right-click the Test Apps node and then choose the "Add App Project" option to browse for the Persons project. Henceforth, you can run UI tests by either pressing the *Run All* button or double-clicking any of the test methods that appear in the Unit Tests pad under the Persons ➤ UITests ➤ Tests node, provided the app was previously deployed to the simulator. A default UI Test App project has only one test method, AppLaunches. If you now execute this method, you will see that the UI Test Framework deploys another app to your simulator, DeviceAgent. DeviceAgent uses the UI automation API provided by the iOS to emulate the gestures and actions that are programmatically defined within your unit tests and send them to the app under test. So, effectively, DeviceAgent acts as a virtual user that, instructed by the test methods, emulates user actions. DeviceAgent also collects the results of these actions and passes them back to the test methods.

To implement test methods, you proceed in a way similar to implementing unit tests. More specifically, every test class is marked by TestFixtureAttribute, while every test method has to be public and decorated by TestAttribute. Listing 6-9 shows that such a structure is utilized in the Tests class—a default test class created with the Persons.UITests project.

Listing 6-9. A Default Definition of the UI Test Class

```
[TestFixture]
public class Tests
{
    iOSApp app;

    [SetUp]
    public void BeforeEachTest()
    {
        app = ConfigureApp.iOS.StartApp();
    }
```

```
    [Test]
    public void AppLaunches()
    {
        app.Screenshot("First screen.");
    }
}
```

By analyzing Listing 6-9, we can easily note two new elements with respect to the unit tests we implemented previously. First and foremost, there is yet another method, BeforeEachTest. This method is marked with a SetUpAttribute. The latter instructs a test runner to invoke a selected function before every test method. Here, BeforeEachTest creates an object that derives from the iOSApp interface. This interface defines methods and properties that you use to interact with the app under test.

To create an object iOSApp, you use the static class ConfigureApp. This class has two properties: Android of type AndroidAppConfigurator, and iOS of type iOSAppConfigurator. For iOS apps, we are only interested in the second one, which is used to configure test parameters (like device identifier, app bundle, and so on). Then, we run tests with the StartApp method. An instance of the iOSApp class is then used to programmatically manipulate the UI in exactly the same way the user would.

To prepare the first UI test for the Persons app, I first extend a definition of the Person class (Persons. Common project) by a static method from Listing 6-10. This method creates an instance of the Person object and then configures the public properties to default values. I will later use the Person.Default method in the UI test and in the Person app.

Listing 6-10. Additional Static Method of the Person Class

```
public static Person Default()
{
    return new Person
    {
        FirstName = "Dawid",
        LastName = "Borycki",
        Age = 34,
        Email = "dawid@borycki.com.pl",
    };
}
```

Next, in the Tests class (Persons.UITests), I implement the VerifyDisplayDataButton test method according to Listing 6-11. VerifyDisplayDataButton virtually taps a button from the view of the Persons app and verifies whether the text in each text field corresponds to the default person data.

To virtually tap a control, you use the Tap method of the iOSApp class instance. This method has two overloaded versions: the one, which accepts as an argument a C# Func delegate, and the other, which accepts string arguments. In the first case, you create the lambda expression, which returns an instance of the AppQuery class. The AppQuery class provides a number of methods that are used to find UI elements. In the second case, you pass a string, which is used by the test runner to find UI elements by inspecting their accessibility identifiers or accessibility labels. Here, to find a button, I use a lambda expression, which I constructed with an AppQuery.Button method. This method matches the first button on the view.

Next, I read text from the text fields using the helper method GetTextFieldText, which finds text fields by their accessibility identifiers. To do so, I construct an AppQuery, in which I pass a string argument representing the control accessibility identifier. Once text from text fields is obtained, I compare it to expected values, and if they differ I raise a corresponding assertion using static methods of the Assert class.

Listing 6-11. UI Test

```
[Test]
public void VerifyDisplayDataButton()
{
    // Arrange
    var defaultPerson = Person.Default();

    // Act
    app.Tap(b => b.Button());

    var actualFirstName = GetTextFieldText("TextFieldFirstName");
    var actualLastName = GetTextFieldText("TextFieldLastName");
    var actualEmail = GetTextFieldText("TextFieldEmail");
    var actualAge = GetTextFieldText("TextFieldAge");

    // Assert
    Assert.AreEqual(defaultPerson.FirstName, actualFirstName);
    Assert.AreEqual(defaultPerson.LastName, actualLastName);
    Assert.AreEqual(defaultPerson.Email, actualEmail);
    Assert.AreEqual(defaultPerson.Age.ToString(), actualAge);

}

private string GetTextFieldText(string textFieldAccessibilityId)
{
    var result = string.Empty;

    if(app.Query(c => c.Id(textFieldAccessibilityId)).FirstOrDefault()
        is AppResult matchedTextField)
    {
        result = matchedTextField.Text;
    }

    return result;
}
```

We can now execute the VerifyDisplayDataButton test method by double-clicking it in the Unit Tests pad. The test runner executes the DeviceAgent, which subsequently runs the Person app and virtually taps a button. Since the corresponding event handler is empty, none of text fields will contain expected values, and the test will fail, which is shown in the Test Results window (Figure 6-17). The Assert.AreEqual method throws an exception, saying that the expected string ("Dawid") differs from the actual one (string.Empty).

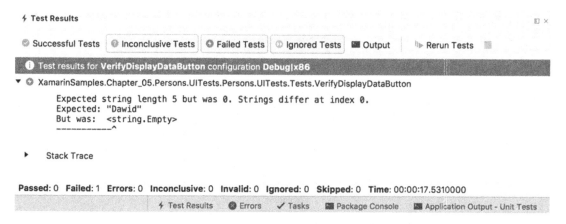

Figure 6-17. *Test Results window*

We can now implement the handler for the `TouchUpInside` event of the button in the Person app according to Listing 6-12 (`ViewController.cs`), rebuild the Person app, and re-run the UI test to confirm the correctness of our implementation. By doing so, we effectively perform a single iteration of the TDD approach. Namely, we first wrote a test method and ran it to verify that the app did not implement expected functionality. We then supplemented an app with the correct logic and re-ran a test method to confirm it. Once test methods are implemented, you can execute them every time you change the related source of code to ensure that you do not introduce regression errors or lose already-implemented functionality. Therefore, such automatic testing helps to develop high-quality apps.

Listing 6-12. A Final Definition of the Event Handler for Displaying Default Person Data

```
partial void ButtonDisplayPersonData_TouchUpInside(UIButton sender)
{
    var defaultPerson = Person.Default();

    TextFieldFirstName.Text = defaultPerson.FirstName;
    TextFieldLastName.Text = defaultPerson.LastName;
    TextFieldAge.Text = defaultPerson.Age.ToString();
    TextFieldEmail.Text = defaultPerson.Email;
}
```

Xamarin Test Cloud

All tests we've written so far were run locally in the simulator. However, the Xamarin UI testing framework can be also utilized to run tests on physical devices. Typically, you deploy an app to be tested to the device and then run UI tests on that device. So, if you need to perform the same tests on various devices, you do it sequentially, which requires extra time. Moreover, you need to physically possess all devices with various OS versions. So, comprehensive testing of an iOS app can be very expensive, especially for individual developers. To solve these problems, Xamarin delivers a farm of physical devices known as the Xamarin Test Cloud. XTC is a cloud-based service to which you can upload an app and its UI tests directly from Visual Studio and then run tests on as many devices as needed. Test results are then presented to you in the form of a clear report, shown previously in Figure 6-4. Although submitting an app to XTC is straightforward, it requires you to create a provisioning profile for your app because an app bundle is executed on physical devices. Hence, I will start this subsection by explaining how to create a provisioning profile, and then I will show you how to submit an app to XTC, choose devices, and execute tests. To complete this section, you will need to create a trial account in the XTC: `https://testcloud.xamarin.com/register`.

Provisioning Profile

To create a provisioning profile, you need Xcode, an Apple ID, and a physical iOS device connected to your development Mac. Then, you proceed as follows:

1. Open Xcode, where you click the Accounts tab. Under Preferences, choose "Apple ID" for type of account, and then type your Apple ID credentials (Figure 6-18). Your account will then appear on the left-hand side of the window, as shown.

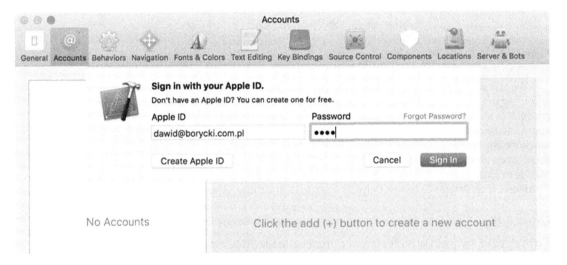

Figure 6-18. *Signing in to Xcode with the Apple ID*

2. Choose your account and click the *Manage Certificates...* button, located in the bottom right part of the Accounts tab (Figure 6-19). This activates the Signing Certificates window.

Figure 6-19. *A list of teams associated with the Apple ID*

3. In the Signing Certificates window, press the + button and choose "iOS Development" (Figure 6-20). Press the *Done* button after a certificate is created, and then press the *Download All or Manual Profiles* button. You can now close Xcode preferences.

Figure 6-20. *Creating a signing certificate*

Given a signing certificate for iOS development, we need to associate it with the Persons app. This needs to be done using Xcode and a physical iOS device connected to the Mac. In Xcode, you now create a new iOS app by going to File ➤ New ➤ Project... A window like that shown in Figure 6-21 appears. In this window, you choose a Single View Application and then click the *Next* button.

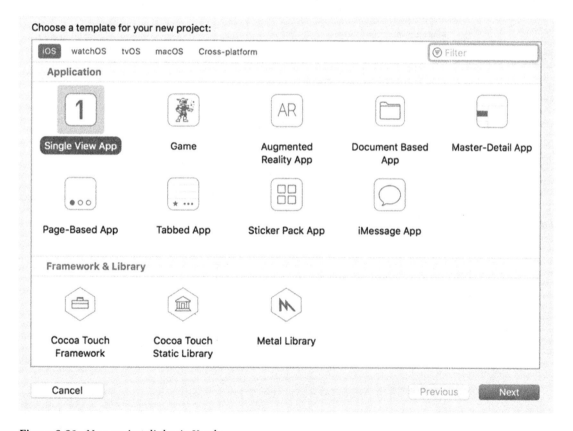

Figure 6-21. *New project dialog in Xcode*

137

After choosing a project template, another window, Choose options for your new project, appears. This window, shown in Figure 6-22, lets you specify the product and organization name for your app. Ensure that these values match the corresponding configuration from the Info.plist of your Xamarin.iOS Person app. Namely, in my case the product name is set to *Persons*, while the organization name is *com.db*. You can leave other options at the default values, then click the *Next* button and choose a location for your project. Xcode will then create an empty app and display its configuration (Figure 6-23). In this window, you need to ensure that the provisioning profile and signing certificate (Signing section) are set. If not, you need to connect a physical iOS device and then press the *Try Again* button, which appears at the bottom of the Signing section.

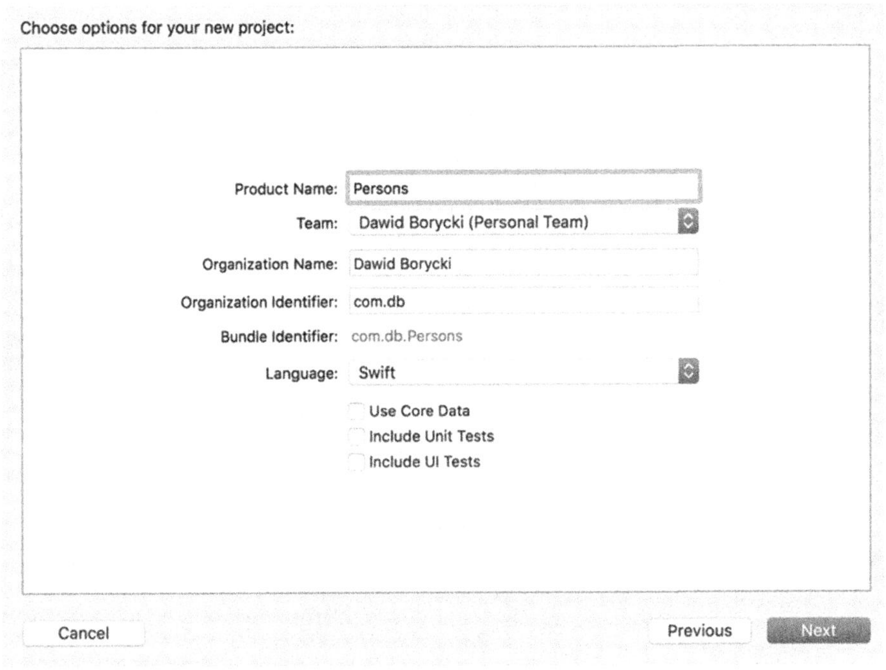

Choose options for your new project:

Product Name:	Persons
Team:	Dawid Borycki (Personal Team)
Organization Name:	Dawid Borycki
Organization Identifier:	com.db
Bundle Identifier:	com.db.Persons
Language:	Swift

- Use Core Data
- Include Unit Tests
- Include UI Tests

Cancel   Previous   Next

Figure 6-22. Configuring project options

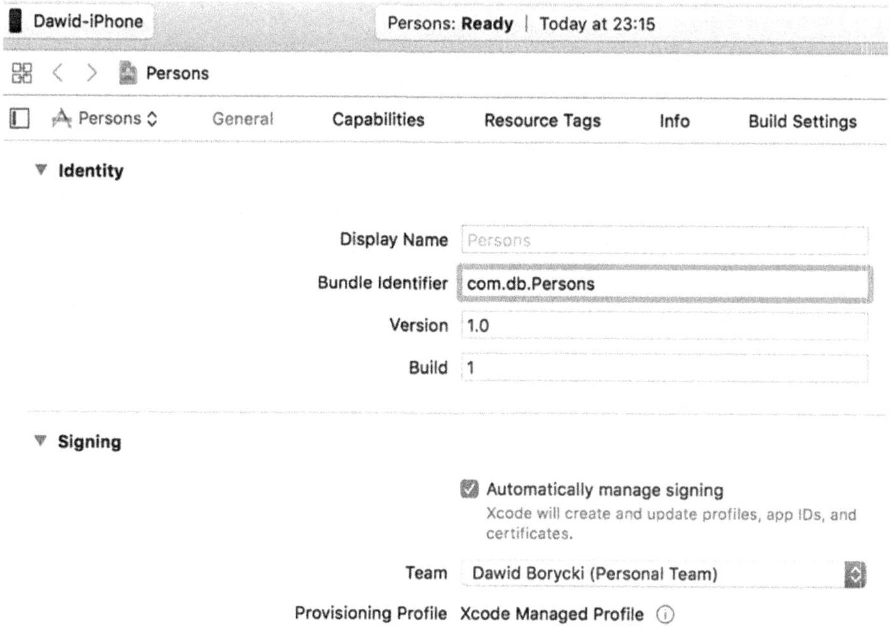

Figure 6-23. *Identity and signing sections of the Persons Xcode app*

Given the provisioning profile, you go back to Visual Studio and open the options of the Persons project (Figure 6-24). Then, go to iOS Bundle Signing under the Build tab, in which you do the following:

- Choose "iPhone" from the Platform drop-down list.

- Set Signing Identity to "Developer (Automatic)."

- Choose "Automatic" from the Provisioning Profile drop-down list.

Figure 6-24. *iOS Bundle Signing section of the Xamarin.iOS Persons app in Visual Studio*

Visual Studio can now generate the app package, which can be deployed to the XTC.

Running Tests in the XTC

To run tests in the XTC, you will eventually need to downgrade the NUnit NuGet package of Persons.UITest. When I was writing this chapter, XTC was supporting NUnit version 2.6.4. The easiest way to downgrade this package is to uninstall it with the "Remove" option of the Package context menu in the Solution Explorer. Then, you re-install a package with the Add Packages window and choose the NUnit version with the drop-down list available in the bottom right part of Package Manager (Figure 6-13).

After ensuring that the NUnit version is compatible with XTC, you go to the Unit Tests pad, right-click the selected UI test, and then choose "Run in Test Cloud." An app will be automatically submitted to the XTC, and after a while you will be automatically redirected to the XTC website. Then, you choose the devices on which tests should be executed. As shown in Figure 6-25, I chose 12 devices, of which 5 are iPads. The others are randomly selected iPhones. Given the list of devices, you then choose Test series (master, production, or beta) and system language, and then press the *Done* button. A test process will be started, and its current status will be displayed on the XTC website (Figure 6-26).

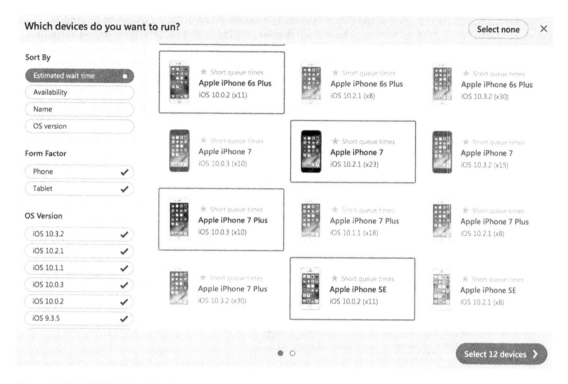

Figure 6-25. *XTC device selection*

Figure 6-26. *Test progress*

Once the tests have completed, you can review the test results for each device using the test report shown earlier in Figure 6-24. In my case, I found that the VerifyDisplayDataButton test method failed on all iPads. According to app screenshots, none of the controls were displayed. I then checked this locally by re-running the Persons app in the iPad simulator. Indeed, none of controls were displayed. However, this is easy to fix with the layout strategies described in Chapter 3. At a minimum, to force the controls to be displayed on larger screens, one must check the "Installed" checkbox of the **wAnyhAny** control property, as shown in Figure 6-27. You can now re-run the tests or run the Persons app in the iPad simulator.

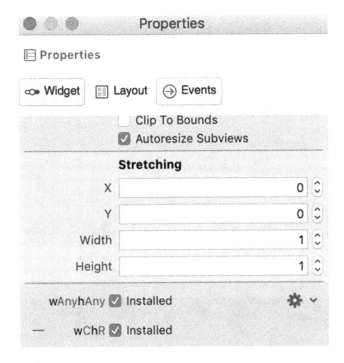

Figure 6-27. *Enabling control visibility for devices of any screen size*

Summary

In this chapter, we explored methods for automatic testing of Xamarin.iOS apps. We started by creating unit tests of the C# code, and then we implemented automatic UI tests. The latter were run locally in the simulator and on multiple physical iOS devices from the Xamarin Test Cloud. You can use all of the presented methods to ensure the high quality of your apps on the very demanding mobile market. We will use the unit testing approach we learned here to develop a client app that consumes and updates data from a web service.

CHAPTER 7

■ ■ ■

Consuming RESTful Web Services

Frequently, iOS apps constitute the mobile endpoint of a larger system. The mobile app retrieves some data, like the weather forecast, news, or bank statements, from a remote web server using RESTful or REST architecture and then displays this data to the user. The user can change or update parts of this data locally and then transfer it to the server. The mobile client can also send requests to the web server; for instance, to execute the money transfer. In this chapter, we will learn how to implement such a mobile client using Xamarin.iOS.

We will use JSONPlaceholder (https://jsonplaceholder.typicode.com/) as the REST web service. It provides several resources that you can use to test your mobile or web app. Here, I'll use the Users resource. It contains a collection of ten objects, each of which represents the hypothetical user object, stored in the JSON format. To see this list, you can type the following URL in your web browser: https://jsonplaceholder.typicode.com/users. You will quickly see that each user is represented by the JSON object shown in Listing 7-1. This object contains several simple type properties, like identifier, name, username, email, phone, and website. There are also two properties of complex types. These are address and company and contain detailed information about the user's address and associated company.

As shown in Figure 7-1, I use this data in the *Users.MobileClient* app to display the list of users in the UITableView. Each table row will contain the user and company name. When you swipe each entry in the list, two row actions will appear: *Remove* and *Details*. The first one will let you remove the particular item from the Users resource. The second action will activate another view, which presents the user's location on the UIMapView as well as two text fields. These will enable you to change the user's name and his or her email address. To implement such functionality, I utilize and combine many topics we learned in previous chapters.

Although the JSONPlaceholder API does not allow you to actually update or remove items from the web service, we can still use it to mimic real interactions with such a web service and update the local data store.

Listing 7-1. JSON Representation of User Object from the JSONPlaceholder

```
{
    "id": 5,
    "name": "Chelsey Dietrich",
    "username": "Kamren",
    "email": "Lucio_Hettinger@annie.ca",
    "address": {
        "street": "Skiles Walks",
        "suite": "Suite 351",
        "city": "Roscoeview",
        "zipcode": "33263",
```

© Dawid Borycki 2018
D. Borycki, *Beginning Xamarin Development for the Mac*, https://doi.org/10.1007/978-1-4842-3132-6_7

```
        "geo": {
            "lat": "-31.8129",
            "lng": "62.5342"
        }
    },
    "phone": "(254)954-1289",
    "website": "demarco.info",
    "company": {
        "name": "Keebler LLC",
        "catchPhrase": "User-centric fault-tolerant solution",
        "bs": "revolutionize end-to-end systems"
    }
}
```

Figure 7-1. *The Users.MobileClient app*

REST Service Client

To implement the Users.MobileClient app, I start by creating the new iOS project using the Single View App template. Then, I add two dependencies, which I will use to communicate with the REST API over the HTTP:

- System.Net.Http, which provides the implementation of the HttpClient class, which I use to communicate with the REST API

- Newtonsoft.Json or Json.NET NuGet package, which implements several classes and methods used to serialize and deserialize JSON objects. More specifically, with this package you can almost automatically map the response received from the web service to the C# object or collection of such objects.

To reference the System.Net.Http assembly, I right-click the References node of the Users.MobileClient app and choose "Edit References," which opens the window shown in Figure 7-2. Subsequently, on the All tab, I check "System.Net.Http."

***Figure 7-2.** Adding a reference to System.Net.Http*

I install the Newtonsoft.Json NuGet package using the Add Packages window, in which I type *Newtonsoft.Json* (Figure 7-3). Then, I check the first item on the list of packages and click the *Add Package* button.

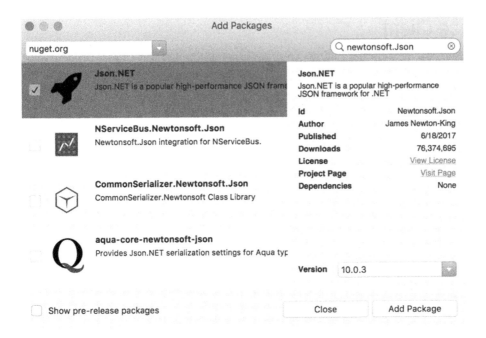

Figure 7-3. *Installing the Newtonsoft.Json aka Json.NET NuGet package*

Given the project and all dependencies are ready, under the Users.MobileClient project, I create the new folder, Helpers, where I add a file, UsersServiceHelper.cs, which stores the static class of the same name. This class, UsersServiceHelper, is used to send requests to the REST API. As Listing 7-2 shows, UsersServiceHelper implements a static constructor that creates the HttpClient class instance. To that end, I use the parameterless constructor of the HttpClient and set its BaseAddress property to the URL of the REST API (Users resource from JSONPlaceholder). Once this is done, you can start sending requests to the REST API using the appropriate methods from the HttpClient class instance. These methods implement corresponding REST verbs. For example, to delete the user you use the DeleteAsync method (Listing 7-3).

Listing 7-2. A Constructor of the UsersServiceHelper Class

```
private static readonly HttpClient httpClient;

static UsersServiceHelper()
{
    httpClient = new HttpClient()
    {
        BaseAddress = new Uri("http://jsonplaceholder.typicode.com/users/")
    };
}
```

Each particular method of the HttpClient class implementing the HTTP requests returns an object of type HttpResponseMessage. The latter, as its name suggests, is an abstract representation of the web server response. So, to check the status of the request and to obtain data returned from the server, you read properties of the HttpResponseMessage. In Listing 7-3, I showed how to check the HTTP status code by accessing the StatusCode property. This property is of type HttpStatusCode enumeration and contains all possible HTTP status codes. To obtain the actual data received from the web service, you use the Content property of type HttpContent. This class represents the body of the HTTP message and has several methods that enable you to read and convert the body to specific formats: string (ReadAsStringAsync method), byte array (ReadAsByteArray async), or stream (ReadAsStreamAsync).

Listing 7-3. Deleting the User

```
public static async Task Delete(int userId)
{
    var response = await httpClient.DeleteAsync($"{userId}");

    CheckStatusCode(response.StatusCode);
}

private static void CheckStatusCode(HttpStatusCode statusCode)
{
    if(statusCode != HttpStatusCode.OK)
    {
        throw new Exception($"Unexpected status code: {statusCode}");
    }
}
```

In Listing 7-4, which shows the Get method of the UsersServiceHelper class, I use the ReadAsStringAsync method because data returned from the web service is written in the JSON format (Listing 7-4). Given that string, I deserialize it to the collection of User .NET objects using the DeserializeObject static method of the JsonConvert class. The latter class comes from Newtonsoft.Json and is the main class that you use to convert between JSON and .NET objects.

Listing 7-4. Retrieving the List of Users from the REST API

```
public static async Task<IEnumerable<User>> Get()
{
    var response = await httpClient.GetAsync(string.Empty);

    CheckStatusCode(response.StatusCode);

    var jsonString = await response.Content.ReadAsStringAsync();

    return JsonConvert.DeserializeObject<IEnumerable<User>>(jsonString);
}
```

Note that in order to convert .NET and C# objects properly you need to implement C# classes whose properties correspond to the appropriate keys in the JSON objects. To make things easier, you can use one of the available online services that generate C# classes based on the JSON object. Here, I use the https://jsonutils.com website, where I paste the JSON object from Listing 7-1 into the JSON text or URL text areas, select C# language, and check "Pascal Case." After pressing the *Submit* button, the website generates four classes: Geo, Address, Company, and Example. I renamed the latter class to User and then stored all of these classes in separate files under the Models folder, which I add to the Users.MobileClient project.

As Listing 7-5 shows, the definition of the User class contains eight auto-implemented public properties that directly correspond to the keys of the JSON object (Listing 7-1). Properties of complex types (Address and Company) are represented by classes of the same names. Their structure is similar to the User class. Namely, they contain appropriate auto-implemented public properties. So, I do not list them here. You can find them in the companion code (Chapter_07/Users.MobileClient/Models).

Listing 7-5. A Definition of the User Class

```
public class User
{
    public int Id { get; set; }
    public string Name { get; set; }
    public string Username { get; set; }
    public string Email { get; set; }
    public Address Address { get; set; }
    public string Phone { get; set; }
    public string Website { get; set; }
    public Company Company { get; set; }
}
```

The only modification I made to these autogenerated classes was to extend the Geo class by another method, ToCLLocationCoordinate2D (Listing 7-6), which converts instances of the Geo class to CLLocationCoordiante2D. I will use this method later to display the user's location on the native map.

Listing 7-6. A Definition of the Geo Class Is Extended by One Public Method

```
using CoreLocation;

namespace Users.MobileClient.Models
{
    public class Geo
    {
        public double Lat { get; set; }
        public double Lng { get; set; }

        public CLLocationCoordinate2D ToCLLocationCoordinate2D()
        {
            return new CLLocationCoordinate2D(Lat, Lng);
        }
    }
}
```

Updating Data

You already know how to delete and retrieve the list of objects from the REST API. You can also update users or add new ones with the PutAsync and PostAsync methods of the HttpClient class, respectively. In both cases, you proceed similarly, so I will only discuss a method of updating user data. Listing 7-7 contains the Update method of the UsersServiceClientHelper class. This method accepts a single argument, an instance of the User class, which contains updated user data. This data is sent to the REST API using the PutAsync method.

Before you can send updated data to the web server, you need to convert or serialize the C# to the JSON object. You do so by using the SerializeObject static method of the JsonConvert class. Then, you send the identifier of the user to be updated and the serialized object. You also need to set the format of the transmitted data: string, byte array, or stream. To that end, you use one of the classes StringContent, ByteArrayContent, or StreamContent, respectively. In Listing 7-7, I show how to use the first of these, which I instantiate with the string returned by the JsonConvert.SerializeObject method. I then put the method from Listing 7-7 in the UsersServiceHelper class.

Listing 7-7. Updating User Data

```
public static async Task Update(User user)
{
    var userJson = JsonConvert.SerializeObject(user);

    var response = await httpClient.PutAsync($"{user.Id}",
        new StringContent(userJson));

    CheckStatusCode(response.StatusCode);
}
```

Getting a Specific User

To get a single user, you need to supplement the GET request with a user identifier. This can be done in a way similar to the case of the Update method from Listing 7-7. In Listing 7-8, I show a complete example of the overloaded UsersServiceClientHelper.Get method, which aims at receiving individual users distinguished by identifiers. It works similarly to the Get method from Listing 7-4 but retrieves only a single User class instance representing the user of a given ID.

Listing 7-8. Retrieving Users by ID

```
public static async Task<User> Get(int userId)
{
    var response = await httpClient.GetAsync($"{userId}");

    CheckStatusCode(response.StatusCode);

    var jsonString = await response.Content.ReadAsStringAsync();

    return JsonConvert.DeserializeObject<User>(jsonString);
}
```

Testing the REST Client

Now, when we have the REST client class implemented we can verify its functionality. Because we already know how to write unit tests, we can test the client class automatically. To create unit tests for UsersServiceClientHelper, I start with a new Unit Test App template and change its name to *Users. MobileClient.Tests*. Then, I edit references such that Users.MobileClient.Tests references the Users. MobileClient project. Subsequently, under the test app, I add a new file, UsersServiceHelperTests.cs, in which I import the following namespaces: System.Linq, System.Threading.Tasks, NUnit.Framework, and Users.MobileClient.Helpers. Then, I declare the UsersServiceHelperTests class as shown in Listing 7-9.

Listing 7-9. A Test Class for the UsersServiceHelper

```
[TestFixture]
public class UsersServiceHelperTests
```

To define the `UsersServiceHelperTests` class, I first create two private members, shown in Listing 7-10. The first one, `UserId`, is a field that stores a default user identifier I will use to validate the `Get` and `Update` methods. The second one is a private function, `GetUserCount`, which calculates the number of elements in a collection of users received from the REST API.

Listing 7-10. Private Members of UsersServiceHelperTest

```
private const int UserId = 5;

private async Task<int> GetUserCount()
{
    return (await UsersServiceHelper.Get()).Count();
}
```

Given the preceding private members, I write the first test method, `VerifyGet`, which validates the number of elements returned by the REST API (Listing 7-11). From the JSONPlaceholder website, I know that the Users resource has ten elements. So, in the `VerifyGet` method, I compare this expected value to that returned by the `GetUserCount` helper from Listing 7-10.

Listing 7-11. Testing a Get Method by Verifying the Number of Returned Elements

```
[Test]
public async void VerifyGet()
{
    // Arrange
    const int expectedDataCount = 10;

    // Act and Assert
    Assert.AreEqual(expectedDataCount, await GetUserCount());
}
```

Next, I implement another test method, `VerifyGetById`, shown in Listing 7-12. This function checks whether two selected public properties of the user retrieved from the REST API possess expected values. Here, I only check the `Name` and `Email` properties of the user with identifier 5.

Listing 7-12. Validating Selected Properties of the User Object Retrieved from the REST API

```
[Test]
public async void VerifyGetById()
{
    // Arrange
    const string expectedName = "Chelsey Dietrich";
    const string expectedEmail = "Lucio_Hettinger@annie.ca";

    // Act
    var user = await UsersServiceHelper.Get(UserId);

    // Assert
    Assert.AreEqual(expectedName, user.Name);
    Assert.AreEqual(expectedEmail, user.Email);
}
```

After writing test methods for the Get functions of the UsersServiceHelper, I implement another two tests, which are shown in Listings 7-13 and 7-14. The first one, VerifyDelete, checks if the number of elements in the Users resource will be decremented after removing one item. To that end, I first read the number of users and store it in the currentDataCount variable. Then, I delete the user of ID 5 and get the user count again. Finally, I check if the actual user count was indeed decremented.

Listing 7-13. Checking if the Delete Method Reduces the Number of Users in the Web Service

```
[Test]
public async void VerifyDelete()
{
    // Arrange
    var currentDataCount = await GetUserCount();
    var expectedDataCount = currentDataCount - 1;

    // Act
    await UsersServiceHelper.Delete(UserId);
    var actualDataCount = await GetUserCount();

    // Assert
    Assert.AreEqual(expectedDataCount, actualDataCount);
}
```

The second method, VerifyUpdate, is used to check whether the UsersServiceHelper.Update method changes the properties of the selected user object in the web service. So, I first get the user of ID 5 and then change its Name property to that stored in the expectedName constant. Then, I invoke the UsersServiceHelper.Update method to request that the web service update the selected user, and then I retrieve the data of this object. Given that user, I read its Name property to see if it was indeed changed as expected. If not, an appropriate assertion will be raised.

Listing 7-14. Validating an Update Method by Checking if It Indeed Changes the Name of the User in the Web Service

```
[Test]
public async void VerifyUpdate()
{
    // Arrange
    const string expectedName = "New name";
    var user = await UsersServiceHelper.Get(UserId);

    // Act
    // Update name of the user and then get the user again from the API
    user.Name = expectedName;
    await UsersServiceHelper.Update(user);
    user = await UsersServiceHelper.Get(UserId);

    // Assert
    // Check if the name of user was indeed updated
    Assert.AreEqual(expectedName, user.Name);
}
```

Given the preceding test methods, I run the Users.MobileService.Tests app in the simulator, and then I execute all four tests. Figure 7-4 features the test app running and the results of our unit tests. We see that only two test methods, VerifyGet and VerifyGetById, were successful. This is because the DELETE and PUT HTTP requests sent to the JSONPlaceholder REST API were faked. The service only returns the OK HTTP status code but does not modify the underlying data. Hence, this functionality will also not work in the mobile client we are going to write. However, we still can modify the data locally and assume that it is correctly updated in the web service.

Figure 7-4. *Unit testing the UsersServiceHelper class*

Users Repository

Given the communication layer is ready, we can now use it in the Users.MobileClient app. As shown in Figure 7-1, Users.MobileClient has two views. Both of them utilize the class implementing a web service client. The first view displays a list of users in the UITableView, while the second view presents more detailed information about the user. Accordingly, there are two view controllers, which will interact with the UsersServiceHelper class. Therefore, I made this class static so it can be easily accessed from various app components. Another approach would be to use the singleton design pattern for the UsersServiceHelper. I'll show you later how to do it with respect to another class, UsersRepository.

There are two more things that should be taken into account when developing a mobile REST API client. First is the local store of the data retrieved from the web service. Second is the data synchronization between the mobile app and the web service. To reduce the number of requests sent to the web service, you typically retrieve the data to a local store when the app starts and then synchronize it with the web service when needed. In advanced scenarios, you perform this synchronization in the background using dedicated worker threads or native background mechanisms.

Here, to implement a local data store or users repository, I create another class, UsersRepository, which I save in the UsersRepository.cs file under the Model folder (see companion code, Chapter_07/ Users.MobileClient/Models). This class serves as the local data store that is synchronized with the remote collection of users. Since UsersRepository will be accessed in several different places of the code and needs to present the same data, I implement this class with a singleton design pattern. This means that UsersRepository will have only one instance, which can be accessed from different places in the source code.

Listing 7-15 shows a fragment of the UsersRepository class, including the following four members:

- Users – a public property that gives other classes access to the collection of users retrieved from the web service

- instance – a private static field that stores a reference to the instance of the UsersRepository class

- GetInstance – a public static method that instantiates the UsersRepository class and saves a reference to it in the instance member. GetInstance also retrieves the list of users from the web service. However, this happens only once, when the instance field is created for the first time. All subsequent calls to the GetInstance method will return a reference to the UsersRepository object

- UsersRepository – a private constructor that prevents the creation of the class from outside. So, callers can only access the privately created instance by invoking the GetInstance method

Listing 7-15. Selected Fragments of the UsersRepository Class

```
public class UsersRepository
{
    public List<User> Users { get; private set; }

    private static UsersRepository instance;

    public static async Task<UsersRepository> GetInstance()
    {
        // Create and initialize an instance only once
        if (instance == null)
        {
            instance = instance ?? new UsersRepository();

            instance.Users = (await UsersServiceHelper.Get()).ToList();
        }

        return instance;
    }

    private UsersRepository()
    {
        // Make default constructor private
        // so the class can be instantiated
        // with the GetInstance method only
    }

    // Definitions of Delete and Update methods
}
```

Subsequently, I extend a definition of the UsersRepository class by three public methods (Listing 7-16):

- GetUserById – retrieves the user from the local data store by user identifier
- Delete – removes the user of the given identifier from the local store and from the remote web service
- Update – updates the user in the local store and in the service

Note that in Listing 7-16 the definitions of the Delete and Update methods are surrounded by the #pragma warning preprocessor directives. This is done to suppress a CS4014 warning, which says: *Because this call is not awaited, execution of the current method continues before the call is completed. Consider applying the 'await' operator to the result of the call.* Here, I intentionally omit the await operator because I do not want to wait for these methods to complete. Instead, I send requests in parallel to speed up updates of the UI.

Listing 7-16. Accessing Data from a Local Store and Data Synchronization with the Remote Web Service

```
public User GetUserById(int userId)
{
    return Users.Find(u => u.Id == userId);
}


#pragma warning disable CS4014

public void Delete(int userId)
{
    if (UserExists(userId))
    {
        var userToDelete = GetById(userId);

        Users.Remove(userToDelete);

        UsersServiceHelper.Delete(userId);
    };
}

public void Update(User user)
{
    if (UserExists(user.Id))
    {
        UsersServiceHelper.Update(user);
    };
}

#pragma warning restore CS4014

private bool UserExists(int userId)
{
    return Users.Exists(u => u.Id == userId);
}
```

Presenting a List of Users

Given the preceding components, I can create the first view, which will present the list of users in a table. To this end, I start by adding to the project another folder, TableSources, where I create a new file, UsersTableSource.cs. It stores a definition of the class UsersTableSource, implementing a source for the users table.

As Listing 7-17 shows, UsersTableSource derives from the UITableViewSource class as does any other class implementing the data source for the UITableView (see Chapter 3). Then, UsersTableSource has two public properties, which store references to the parent view controller (used for navigation) and users repository, respectively. As explained in Chapter 3, UsersTableSource has to override several base methods. In particular, it should override the GetCell method, which is used to display elements of the list. Here, this method first retrieves an instance of the User class from the repository. This object contains the user data to be displayed in a given row. The row index path is related to the user identifier, so I use this path to retrieve users from the repository using the GetById method (Listing 7-16). To convert a row index path to a user identifier, I utilize a helper method, GetUserId, seen in Listing 7-17. Given the User class instance, I create or reuse the cell of style UITableViewCellStyle.Value1. Finally, I configure the Text properties of the TextLabel and DetailTextLabel such that they display the name of the user and the name of his or her company (refer back to Figure 7-1).

Listing 7-17. A Fragment of UsersTableSource Class

```
public class UsersTableSource : UITableViewSource
{
    public UIViewController ParentViewController { get; set; }
    public UsersRepository UsersRepository { get; set; }

    private const string cellId = "UserCell";

    public override UITableViewCell GetCell(
        UITableView tableView, NSIndexPath indexPath)
    {
        // Get item to display
        var user = UsersRepository.GetById(GetUserId(indexPath));

        // Try to reuse a cell before creating a new one
        var cell = tableView.DequeueReusableCell(cellId)
            ?? new UITableViewCell(UITableViewCellStyle.Value1, cellId);

        // Configure cell properties
        cell.TextLabel.Text = user.Name;
        cell.DetailTextLabel.Text = user.Company.Name;

        return cell;
    }

    private int GetUserId(NSIndexPath indexPath)
    {
        return UsersRepository.Users[indexPath.Row].Id;
    }

    // The rest of class definition
}
```

I now add row actions representing two buttons, which appear when the user swipes an element in a table (refer back to Figure 7-1). As Listing 7-18 shows, the first button has a *Remove* caption and will invoke the DeleteUser method whenever user taps it. The second button has the *Details* caption and is used to present a second view with user details and his or her location on the map using the DisplayUserDetails helper method.

Listing 7-18. Creating Row Actions

```
public override UITableViewRowAction[] EditActionsForRow(
    UITableView tableView, NSIndexPath indexPath)
{
    var removeButton = UITableViewRowAction.Create(
        UITableViewRowActionStyle.Destructive,
        "Remove",
        delegate
        {
            DeleteUser(tableView, indexPath);
        });

    var detailsButton = UITableViewRowAction.Create(
        UITableViewRowActionStyle.Normal,
        "Details",
        delegate
        {
            DisplayUserDetails(tableView, indexPath);
        });

    return new UITableViewRowAction[] { removeButton, detailsButton };
}
```

To delete the user, in the UsersTableSource class I implement a DeleteUser method, shown in Listing 7-19. This function first removes the user from the repository, and then the item from the list.

Listing 7-19. Deleting the User

```
private void DeleteUser(UITableView tableView, NSIndexPath indexPath)
{
    UsersRepository.Delete(GetUserId(indexPath));

    tableView.DeleteRows(RowIndexToArray(indexPath),
        UITableViewRowAnimation.Automatic);
}

private NSIndexPath[] RowIndexToArray(NSIndexPath indexPath)
{
    return new NSIndexPath[] { indexPath };
}
```

A definition of the DisplayUserDetails method appears in Listing 7-20. This function instantiates the UserDetailsViewController, which is associated with the second view shown on the right part of Figure 7-1. Then, I use the User property of this view controller to pass the data for the current user from the first to the second view. Finally, I perform a navigation to the second view with the PresentViewController method of the UIViewController class. After the navigation is done, I reload the current row so the action buttons do not appear when the app user navigates back to the first view.

Listing 7-20. Displaying User Details

```
private void DisplayUserDetails(
    UITableView tableView, NSIndexPath indexPath)
{
    // Instantiate view controller
    var userDetailsViewController = ParentViewController.
        Storyboard.InstantiateViewController("UserDetailsViewController")
        as UserDetailsViewController;

    // Pass selected user
    userDetailsViewController.User =
        UsersRepository.GetById(GetUserId(indexPath));

    // Present view controller
    ParentViewController.PresentViewController(
        userDetailsViewController,
        true,
        () => ReloadRow(tableView, indexPath));
}

private void ReloadRow(UITableView tableView, NSIndexPath indexPath)
{
    var indexes = RowIndexToArray(indexPath);

    tableView.ReloadRows(indexes, UITableViewRowAnimation.None);
}
```

Now, when the table source is ready, I can use it to create the UITableView and display it in the first app view. Before I do this, in the iOS designer, I use the properties of the view controller to set its class to UsersListViewController, and then I remove the ViewController.cs file, as it is not necessary. Subsequently, in the UsersListViewController, I declare the following private members (Listing 7-21):

- usersTable of type UITableView, which stores a reference to the table

- AddUsersTable, which creates and configures the table

- GetFrameWithVerticalMargin, a method that adds a constant top margin to the view frame to save space for the iOS status bar

Listing 7-21. Creating a Table and Presenting a List of Users

```
private UITableView usersTable;

private async Task AddUsersTable()
{
    var usersTableSource = new UsersTableSource()
    {
        ParentViewController = this,
        UsersRepository = await UsersRepository.GetInstance()
    };
```

```
    usersTable = new UITableView(GetFrameWithVerticalMargin(20))
    {
        Source = usersTableSource
    };

    Add(usersTable);
}

private CGRect GetFrameWithVerticalMargin(nfloat offset)
{
    var rect = View.Frame;

    rect.Y = offset;
    rect.Height -= offset;

    return rect;
}
```

Then, I modify the ViewDidLoad and ViewWillAppear view event handlers according to Listing 7-22. Namely, I use ViewDidLoad to create and display a table, while in ViewWillAppear I reload the data in the table so that it will include all eventual updates that the app user can make using the second view.

Listing 7-22. View Event Handlers of UsersListViewController

```
public override async void ViewDidLoad()
{
    base.ViewDidLoad();

    await AddUsersTable();
}

public override void ViewWillAppear(bool animated)
{
    base.ViewWillAppear(animated);

    usersTable?.ReloadData();
}
```

Displaying User Details

After ensuring the first view is ready, we can move forward and create the second view, which shows user details. To this end, I use the iOS designer, where I drag from the toolbox a new view controller. Subsequently, I set its class to UserDetailsViewController, and design its view, as shown in the right part of Figure 7-1. I also change the names of selected controls in the view as follows:

- The name of the first text field is TextFieldName.

- The name of the second text field is TextFieldEmail.

- The name of the MKMapView control is MapViewAddress.

- The first button is named ButtonCancel.

- The second button is named ButtonUpdate.

Once this is done, I implement the logic. First, in the UserDetailsViewController class, I declare one public property, User, and two private fields (Listing 7-23). The property is used to pass the user data to be displayed. The first field configures the region of the map, and the second field stores a reference to the UsersRepository object.

Listing 7-23. A Fragment of the UserDetailsViewController Class

```
public partial class UserDetailsViewController : UIViewController
{
    public User User { get; set; }

    private const double spanDelta = 0.05d;

    private UsersRepository usersRepository;

    // Further class definition
}
```

Then, I implement the ViewDidLoad event handler as shown in Listing 7-24. Namely, I obtain the instance of the UsersRepository class and then configure the map such that it can be scrolled and zoomed.

Listing 7-24. Obtaining an Instance of the UsersRepository and Map Configuration

```
public override async void ViewDidLoad()
{
    base.ViewDidLoad();

    usersRepository = await UsersRepository.GetInstance();

    MapViewAddress.ScrollEnabled = true;
    MapViewAddress.ZoomEnabled = true;
}
```

Given that this part is ready, I can display the user's name, email address, and location in the view. I use the ViewWillAppear view event handler (Listing 7-25). I extend the base implementation of this event handler by two statements invoking the following methods: DisplayUserData and UpdateMap. As shown in Listing 7-25, the first one is utilized to update the Text properties of text fields so that they present the name and email address of the user. The second method, which I will discuss shortly, takes the user's geolocation and presents it on the map.

Listing 7-25. Displaying User Details

```
public override void ViewWillAppear(bool animated)
{
    base.ViewWillAppear(animated);

    DisplayUserData();

    UpdateMap(User.Address.Geo.ToCLLocationCoordinate2D());
}
```

```
private void DisplayUserData()
{
    TextFieldName.Text = User.Name;
    TextFieldEmail.Text = User.Email;
}
```

As a next step, I create TouchUpInside event handlers for two buttons and then implement them according to Listing 7-26. The first event handler associated with ButtonCancel is used to navigate back to the first view without making any changes to the user's data, unlike the second event handler, which first updates these data according to changes made by the app user (see UpdateUserData method from Listing 7-26).

Listing 7-26. TouchUpInside Event Handlers for Buttons

```
partial void ButtonCancel_TouchUpInside(UIButton sender)
{
    DismissViewController(true, null);
}

partial void ButtonUpdate_TouchUpInside(UIButton sender)
{
    UpdateUserData();

    ButtonCancel_TouchUpInside(sender);
}

private void UpdateUserData()
{
    User.Name = TextFieldName.Text;
    User.Email = TextFieldEmail.Text;

    usersRepository.Update(User);
}
```

Finally, I update the map view using a set of methods from Listing 7-27. I used similar methods previously in Chapter 3. So, I do not repeat this discussion. The only new thing is the AddPin method, which creates the pin annotation on the map.

Listing 7-27. Displaying User's Geolocation on the Map

```
private void UpdateMap(CLLocationCoordinate2D centerCoordinate)
{
    AddPin(centerCoordinate);

    SetMapRegion(centerCoordinate);
}

private void SetMapRegion(CLLocationCoordinate2D centerCoordinate)
{
    var span = new MKCoordinateSpan(spanDelta, spanDelta);

    var region = new MKCoordinateRegion(centerCoordinate, span);
```

```
        MapViewAddress.SetRegion(region, false);
}

private void AddPin(CLLocationCoordinate2D centerCoordinate)
{
    var pin = new PinMapAnnotation(centerCoordinate, User.Name);

    MapViewAddress.AddAnnotation(pin);
}
```

To create an annotation, you first implement a class deriving from the MKAnnotation and then add instances of your class to the map using the AddAnnotation method of the MKMapView class instance (refer back to the AddPin method from Listing 7-27). Listing 7-28 shows a full definition of the PinMapAnnotation class, which I use to create a simple pin annotation. PinMapAnnotation has two private fields: *coordinate* and *title*. The first one represents the pin location, while the other is a title displayed in the popup that appears when you tap the pin. There are also three methods associated with these fields. These methods, which are derived from the base class, are the following: Coordinate, SetCoordinate, and Title. The first two methods are used to get and set coordinates, while the last method is used to get the title value. The last element of the PinMapAnnotation is the class constructor, which accepts two arguments. Their values are stored in the appropriate private members of the class.

Listing 7-28. Implementation of the Pin Map Annotation

```
public class PinMapAnnotation : MKAnnotation
{
    private CLLocationCoordinate2D coordinate;
    private readonly string title;

    public override CLLocationCoordinate2D Coordinate
    {
        get => coordinate;
    }

    public override void SetCoordinate(CLLocationCoordinate2D value)
    {
        coordinate = value;
    }

    public override string Title
    {
        get => title;
    }

    public PinMapAnnotation(CLLocationCoordinate2D coordinate, string title)
    {
        this.coordinate = coordinate;
        this.title = title;
    }
}
```

Now, you can compile and execute the app in the simulator. You will quickly see the first view, which presents the list of users. You can swipe each element to activate row actions. Use them to either update or remove users.

Summary

In this chapter, we learned how to implement a Xamarin.iOS app that interacts with a web service over the HTTP protocol. To that end, we utilized the `HttpClient` class from the `System.Net.Http` assembly and implemented a class to consume and send data from and to the remote RESTful service. We also created a local data store, which was synchronized with remote resources. Subsequently, we created unit tests to automatically validate the correctness of our implementations. Finally, we created the app, which displays information retrieved from the remote service. Because the `HttpClient` class is also available for other platforms, including Universal Windows Platform and Android.iOS, we could also use techniques presented here to develop REST API clients for those platforms. This chapter ends our exciting adventure with iOS apps. In the next chapter, we will learn how to create apps for a wearable Apple Watch platform.

CHAPTER 8

■ ■ ■

watchOS

Apple Watch is a smartwatch equipped with multiple sensors supporting health and activity data tracking. Moreover, Apple Watch contains communication interfaces, making it a wearable endpoint of the iOS device. The smartwatch becomes your best friend when riding a bike, when at an important meeting, or when standing on a crowded bus. In such situations, you cannot pull out the phone. Instead, you can use your Apple Watch to quickly check your schedule, reply to incoming messages, or glance at the map to see route directions.

Apple Watch is controlled by the dedicated operating system watchOS. There are several generations of this OS. The first one, watch OS 1, is already deprecated, and new solutions should target at least watchOS 2. When I was writing this chapter, Visual Studio for Mac and Xamarin.iOS were supporting watchOS 2 and above.

You can develop custom apps for watchOS using the dedicated SDK. In practice, you do this quite similarly to how you develop iOS apps. However, there is a difference between the watchOS and iOS; namely, watch apps comprise two bundles. The first one is the actual watch app, which contains the user interfaces. The other bundle, watch or WatchKit extension, implements a logic controlling the UI. So, most of the time you modify the storyboard of the watch app and implement logic by modifying the definitions of classes representing controllers that are associated with the UI. This is done using the WatchKit framework, which is a set of classes that helps you control watchOS app.

In this chapter, I will guide you through this process starting from the ground up. We will first create the project and then analyze its structure, learning about the most important features of watchOS apps.

Creating the Project

Every watchOS app has an associated iOS app. Therefore, to implement the first watchOS solution, I start by creating the parent app, *HelloWatchKit*, using Single View App iOS project template. I set the target version to iOS 11.0. Then, I create the actual watchOS app with the WatchKit App project template. The latter is available under the watchOS group (Figure 8-1). After choosing a template, I press the *Next* button, which activates another window in which, similar to the iOS case, you can configure your new watchOS app.

© Dawid Borycki 2018
D. Borycki, *Beginning Xamarin Development for the Mac*, https://doi.org/10.1007/978-1-4842-3132-6_8

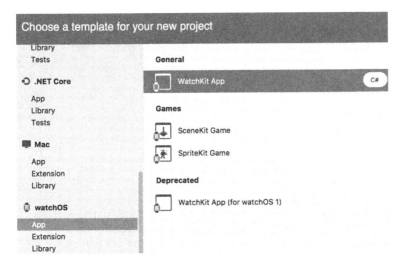

Figure 8-1. *A list of project templates for creating watchOS apps*

As Figure 8-2 shows, to configure the watchOS app you specify the following attributes:

- Project – which indicates the parent iOS project. Here, I set it to *HelloWatchKit*.

- App Name – I set it to *Watch*. When typing the name of your watch app, keep in mind that it will be preceded by the name of your parent iOS app. For instance, for HelloWatchKit, watchOS projects will be named *HelloWatchKit.Watch* and *HelloWatchKit.WatchExtension*. As we will quickly see, the first one defines the UI of the watch app and the latter contains associated logic.

- Target – the minimum watchOS version that your app will support. I set it to watchOS 2.0, which is officially the minimum watchOS version available.

- Scenes – a list of scenes for your watchOS app. Here, I checked all possible scenes and will discuss them later in this chapter.

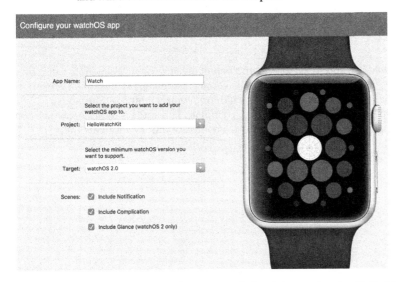

Figure 8-2. *Configuring the watchOS app such that it is associated with the HelloWatchKit iOS parent app*

After creating the project, you will see that the whole solution comprises three projects, as follows:

- *HelloWatchKit* – the parent iOS app. This is the only app that your watchOS app can communicate with. This project references *HelloWatchKit.Watch*.

- *HelloWatchKit.Watch* – a bundle that contains storyboards for the watchOS app and references *HelloWatchKit.WatchExtension*.

- *HelloWatchKit.WatchExtension* – a bundle that stores logic (the app's code) and resources.

Since we already know the structure of the iOS app, let's briefly investigate the last two bundles.

Watch App Bundle

A quick glance at HelloWatchKit.Watch reveals that its structure is composed of three files. There are two property lists (Info and Entitlements) and the `Interface.storyboard`. After opening the latter in the iOS designer, you will see that it contains four scenes. Similar to the iOS case, these scenes represent views with content. The number of scenes depends on what we configured in Figure 8-2. Therefore, apart from the initial scene, we have notification and glance scenes.

Once in the iOS designer (Figure 8-3), you can visually design each scene by dragging controls from the toolbox. Note that the list of available controls is different than what we saw when working with iOS apps. The toolbox now contains controls that are tailored to the physical limitations of the Apple Watch.

In the watchOS app, controllers associated with views are defined as interface controllers instead of view controllers as in iOS. Each scene has an associated interface controller, which is defined in the HelloWatchKit.WatchExtension and, as we will quickly see, derives from the `WKInterfaceController` class of the WatchKit. `WKInterfaceController` is the base class for all interface controllers. This class is the watch counterpart of the `UIViewController` from the iOS app. However, unlike the `UIViewController`, the `WKInterfaceController` does not directly manage any views. Instead, it remotely (from a different bundle) interfaces with and controls the behavior of the storyboard defined in the Watch bundle.

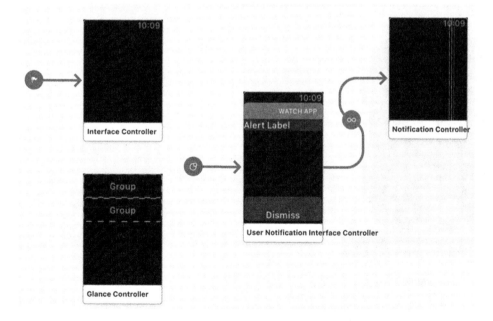

Figure 8-3. A default storyboard of the watchOS app

Watch Extension

The watch extension bundle is implemented within HelloWatchKit.WatchExtension. If you expand this project in the Solution pad, you will quickly see that it contains several files that implement interface controllers. This file set includes the following items:

- `InterfaceController.cs` – This file stores a definition of the `InterfaceController` class. The latter implements the logic associated with the default or initial scene of the HelloWatchKit.Watch app. Therefore, `InterfaceController` is analogous to the default `ViewController` we used while developing iOS apps.

- `NotificationController.cs` – This contains a definition of the `NotificationController`, which manages notifications.

- `ComplicationController.cs` – This stores a definition of the `ComplicationController` used to define small visual elements (complications) that are shown directly on the watch face.

- `GlanceController.cs` – This contains a definition of the `GlanceController` class, which is used to control the glance scene.

There is also one other important file, `ExtensionDelegate.cs`. It stores a definition of the `ExtensionDelegate` class, which is somewhat analogous to the `AppDelegate` class used by the iOS apps. I will tell you later how you can utilize the preceding classes while developing apps for the watchOS.

Hello, Watch!

Let's now use the watch and watch extension bundles to implement a custom timer, as shown in Figure 8-4. To this end, I first open the Watch app bundle project and modify the first scene by adding a label. I then set the label name to LabelTime and center it vertically and horizontally by choosing the center option from the Horizontal and Vertical Alignment drop-down lists. They are located under the View group.

Figure 8-4. *A view of the watchOS app*

Subsequently, I go to the WatchExtension bundle and edit InterfaceController.cs. I first import the System.Timers namespace and then extend a definition of the InterfaceController class such that a current time will be presented in the label. Therefore, I will repeatedly obtain the current system time and display it in the label. To implement such a functionality, you typically use the System.Timers.Timer class. It implements a mechanism, which lets you execute a method at specified intervals. You specify the interval by setting the Interval property of the Timer class instance. Once this is done and the timer is started (Start method), it will raise an Elapsed event. To execute your custom logic, all you need to do is handle that event. Because this event is invoked on the UI thread, you do not need to worry about thread safety when accessing visual controls from the Timer.Elapsed event handler, as discussed in Chapter 3.

In Listing 8-1, I show one private field and three private methods, which I use to implement the digital watch. The first function, ConfigureTimer, is used to create an instance of the Timer class, which is stored in the Timer field. Here, the Timer class is used to repeatedly execute a DisplayCurrentTime method at one-second intervals. This method reads and formats the current time and then displays it in the label with the SetText method. In Listing 8-1, I also include a method for starting and stopping the timer (UpdateTimer).

Listing 8-1. Using a Timer to Present Current Time

```
private Timer timer;

private void ConfigureTimer()
{
    if(timer == null)
    {
        timer = new Timer();

        timer.Elapsed += (sender, e) =>
        {
            DisplayCurrentTime();
        };

        timer.Interval = 1000;
    }
}

private void DisplayCurrentTime()
{
    var time = String.Format("{0:HH:mm:ss}", DateTime.Now);

    LabelTime.SetText(time);
}

private void UpdateTimer(bool start = true)
{
    if(start)
    {
        DisplayCurrentTime();
        timer.Start();
    }
    else
    {
        timer.Stop();
    }
}
```

I then use the ConfigureTimer and UpdateTimer methods in the view event handlers of InterfaceController. By default, there are three such methods implemented: Awake, WillActivate, and DidDeactivate. They override the base implementations of the corresponding methods from the WKInterfaceController, and, similar to iOS, correspond to the view lifecycle. The first method, Awake, is invoked by the runtime shortly after initializing the interface controller. So, you use this method to customize the initialization process. Therefore, the Awake method is a good place to create and configure the timer. Thus, as shown in Listing 8-2, I invoke the ConfigureTimer method there. Also, I use the SetTitle method there, which changes the string displayed in the view header (see Figure 8-4).

Listing 8-2. Configuring a Timer

```
public override void Awake(NSObject context)
{
    base.Awake(context);

    SetTitle("Hello, watch!");

    ConfigureTimer();

    Console.WriteLine("{0} awake with context", this);
}
```

Once the timer is set up, I can start and stop it when the interface controller is about to become active or inactive, respectively (Listing 8-3). Any attempts to update the interface controller when it is inactive are ignored by the runtime.

Listing 8-3. Starting and Stopping a Timer

```
public override void WillActivate()
{
    UpdateTimer();

    Console.WriteLine("{0} will activate", this);
}

public override void DidDeactivate()
{
    UpdateTimer(false);

    Console.WriteLine("{0} did deactivate", this);
}
```

Now, you can run the watch app in one of the simulators. As shown in Figure 8-5, to choose the simulator use the Debug Target drop-down list in Visual Studio. Here, I use Apple Watch Series 3 – 42 mm watchOS 4.0. Also note that you have three possible options for how to execute the HelloWatchKit.Watch app. Depending on this choice, a different interface controller will be used to initialize the app. The possible run options include a default (HelloWatchKit.Watch), glance (HelloWatchKit.Watch – Glance), and notification (HelloWatchKit.Watch – Notification) items. For now, choose a default one and run the app. Two simulators will be started. The first iOS simulator runs in order to execute the parent iOS app. The second emulates the paired Apple Watch and executes the watchOS app shown previously in Figure 8-4. Note that, depending on the Apple Watch simulator you choose, a different iOS simulator will be used. Each Watch simulator is paired with only one iPhone simulator. You can configure this pairing in the Xcode by going to the Hardware ➤ Device ➤ Manage Devices option from the Hardware menu of any simulator.

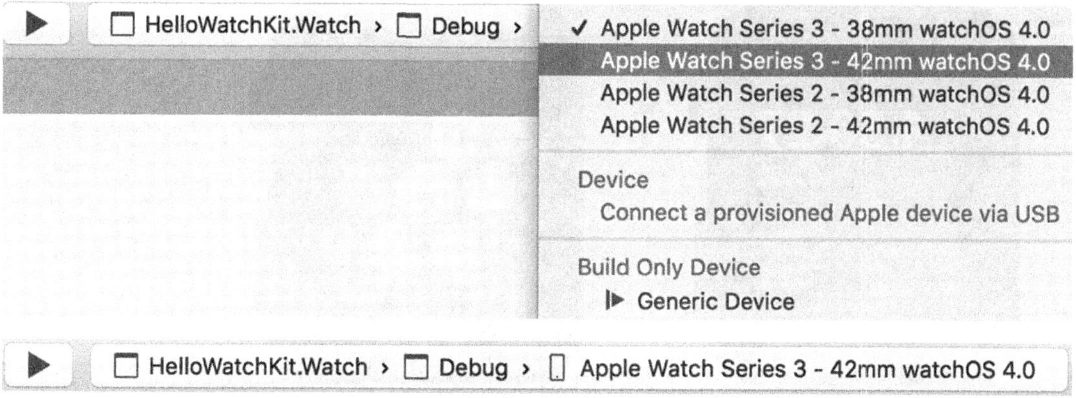

Figure 8-5. *Choosing the Apple Watch simulator*

Watch Simulator

After implementing and running the first watchOS app, it is a good time to stop and learn how to control the Apple Watch simulator so we can test various app functionalities. The Apple Watch simulator can be controlled in much the same way as the iPhone simulator. Specifically, when you turn on the simulator it will present the screen shown in the top left corner of Figure 8-6. That is the watch face. You can change this face by swiping left or right. Once in the watch face, you can tap one of complications (small icons shown at the top or bottom of the screen). You can also go to the home screen by pressing SHIFT+COMMAND+H. The home screen, shown in the top right corner of Figure 8-6, contains a series of circular icons representing apps. The upper one is associated with the HelloWatchKit.Watch app we created. So, when you tap it, this app becomes active. You can use the home screen to run any other app, like Settings, for instance (see bottom left part of Figure 8-6). To switch between apps, you use the dock (bottom right part of Figure 8-6), which you can activate in the simulator by pressing SHIFT+COMMAND+B or press the side button of the Apple Watch simulator. Once the dock is shown, you can choose the app to activate (by swiping left or right) or close it by swiping up and then pressing the Remove icon. A real Apple Watch is also equipped with the digital crown, used to scroll between various options. To use the digital crown in the simulator, you use the mouse scroll or appropriate gesture on your touchpad.

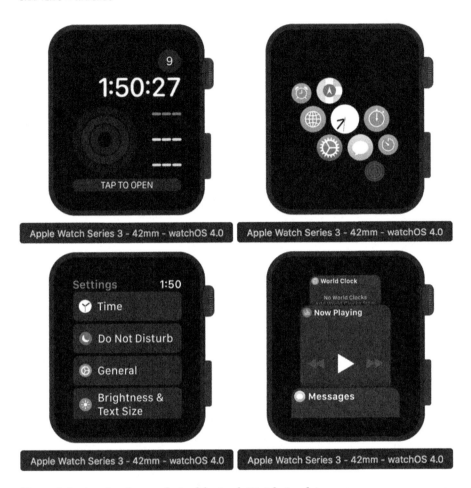

Figure 8-6. *A series of screenshots of the Apple Watch simulator*

You can also personalize the Apple Watch from the paired iPhone. To do so, you use the Apple Watch app on the parent device. Figure 8-7 shows an example of how to use Apple Watch app to change the watch face.

Figure 8-7. *Configuring the watch from the associated iPhone*

View Lifecycle

After getting familiar with the Apple Watch simulator and the app structure, let's go further and investigate the view (or interface) controller lifecycle. As I mentioned previously, this lifecycle is accompanied by several events you can customize with the appropriate view event handlers. These handlers are defined in the WKInterfaceController class, so to implement custom logic you need to override them in the derived class. To present an example, I modify the InterfaceController by importing the System.Diagnostics namespace and implementing the DisplayInfo method from Listing 8-4. Then, I invoke this method in five view event handlers (Listing 8-5): Awake, WillActivate, DidDeactivate, DidAppear, and WillDisappear.

Listing 8-4. Displaying the Name of the View Event

```
private void DisplayInfo(string eventName)
{
    Debug.WriteLine($"{this.Class.Name}, view event: {eventName}");
}
```

Listing 8-5. Tracking the View Lifecycle

```
public override void Awake(NSObject context)
{
    base.Awake(context);

    SetTitle("Hello, watch!");

    ConfigureTimer();

    DisplayInfo("Awake");
}

public override void WillActivate()
{
    UpdateTimer();

    DisplayInfo("WillActivate");
}

public override void DidDeactivate()
{
    UpdateTimer(false);

    DisplayInfo("DidDeactivate");
}

public override void DidAppear()
{
    DisplayInfo("DidAppear");
}

public override void WillDisappear()
{
    DisplayInfo("WillDisappear");
}
```

To see when the preceding event handlers are invoked during the view lifecycle, I re-run the HelloWatchKit.Watch app and open the application output (Figure 8-8). When the app is started, the runtime invokes the following view event handlers sequentially: Awake, WillActivate, and DidAppear. This means that the interface controller is first initialized and configured, then the view is activated and shown on the screen of the smartwatch. Subsequently, I go to the home screen. As a result, the app is deactivated and its view disappears. This is associated with five events: DidDeactivate, WillActivate, DidAppear, WillDisappear, and DidDeactivate. We see that right after the app is deactivated it becomes active and visible for a short while (WillActivate and DidAppear view events are raised). This is done only by watchOS 3.0 and above to take a snapshot of the current app state. The watchOS takes the app snapshot to present it in the Dock. After the snapshot is taken, the view of the app becomes invisible (WillDisappear) and the app is deactivated (DidDeactivate).

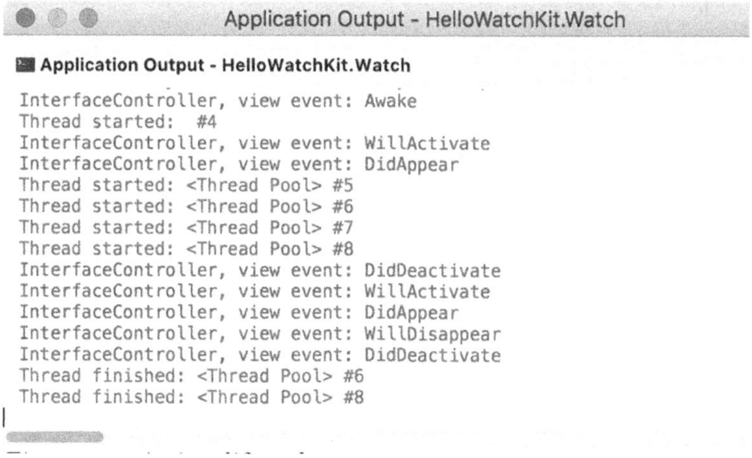

```
● ● ●         Application Output - HelloWatchKit.Watch

■ Application Output - HelloWatchKit.Watch
InterfaceController, view event: Awake
Thread started:  #4
InterfaceController, view event: WillActivate
InterfaceController, view event: DidAppear
Thread started: <Thread Pool> #5
Thread started: <Thread Pool> #6
Thread started: <Thread Pool> #7
Thread started: <Thread Pool> #8
InterfaceController, view event: DidDeactivate
InterfaceController, view event: WillActivate
InterfaceController, view event: DidAppear
InterfaceController, view event: WillDisappear
InterfaceController, view event: DidDeactivate
Thread finished: <Thread Pool> #6
Thread finished: <Thread Pool> #8
```

Figure 8-8. *A view lifecycle*

App Lifecycle

You now know how to handle view event handlers. So, we can now learn how to implement custom logic for handling the watchOS app lifecycle. To this end, you subclass the WKExtensionDelegate class. In the HelloWatchKit.WatchExtension app we already have an ExtensionDelegate.cs file containing a definition of the class deriving from WKExtensionDelegate. This class, ExtensionDelegate, serves a similar purpose as AppDelegate (a subclass of the UIApplicationDelegate) in iOS apps. More specifically, you use ExtensionDelegate to handle the app's execution state changes using associated events. To show the execution order of these events, I modify the ExtensionDelegate.cs file, where I first import the System. Diagnostics namespace and then supplement a definition of the ExtensionDelegate class by the two private methods from Listing 8-6. The first one, DisplayInfo, is used to write an event name to the application output. The second one, IsEventSupported, is used to check the watchOS version. This is a helper that I use to ensure that the specific event handlers can be utilized.

Listing 8-6. Outputting Event Name to the Application Output and Checking watchOS Version

```
private void DisplayInfo(string eventName)
{
    Debug.WriteLine($"App event: {eventName}");
}

private bool IsEventSupported()
{
    return WKInterfaceDevice.CurrentDevice.CheckSystemVersion(3, 0);
}
```

I then use the preceding methods to implement five app event handlers as shown in Listing 8-7. Note that I check for watchOS version in two of them—ApplicationWillEnterForeground and ApplicationDidEnterBackground—because they are only available in watchOS 3.0 or later. Otherwise, the DisplayInfo will not be invoked for that two event handlers.

Listing 8-7. Tracking the App Lifecycle

```
public override void ApplicationDidFinishLaunching()
{
    DisplayInfo("ApplicationDidFinishLaunching");
}

public override void ApplicationDidBecomeActive()
{
    DisplayInfo("ApplicationDidBecomeActive");
}

public override void ApplicationWillResignActive()
{
    DisplayInfo("ApplicationWillResignActive");
}

public override void ApplicationWillEnterForeground()
{
    if (IsEventSupported())
    {
        DisplayInfo("ApplicationWillEnterForeground");
    }
}

public override void ApplicationDidEnterBackground()
{
    if (IsEventSupported())
    {
        DisplayInfo("ApplicationDidEnterBackground");
    }
}
```

I now re-run the app and open the Application Output pad to see when the preceding event handlers are invoked during the runtime. As shown in Figure 8-9, this output, in addition to the strings describing view event handlers, contains entries about the app view lifecycle. We can see that two app events, ApplicationDidFinishLaunching and ApplicationDidBecomeActive, are raised after initialization of the interface controller (Awake view event handler). Then, the interface controller is activated and displayed.

Subsequently, I go to the home screen. As a result, the watch app becomes inactive and is put into the background. This is accompanied by two app events, ApplicationWillResignActive and ApplicationDidEnterBackground, respectively. After these app events, five view events are raised, which we have analyzed already. Let's now see what happens if we re-activate the app from the home screen. This will cause watchOS to fire another two app events: ApplicationWillEnterForeground and ApplicationDidBecomeActive. So, you now know the exact order of app and view events, which you can use to write custom logic handling various states of your app and interface controllers.

```
● ● ○            Application Output - HelloWatchKit.Watch

■ Application Output - HelloWatchKit.Watch                              □ ×

InterfaceController, view event: Awake
Thread started:  #4
InterfaceController, view event: WillActivate
InterfaceController, view event: DidAppear
Thread started: <Thread Pool> #5
Thread started: <Thread Pool> #6
Thread started: <Thread Pool> #7
Thread started: <Thread Pool> #8
App event: ApplicationWillResignActive
App event: ApplicationDidEnterBackground
InterfaceController, view event: DidDeactivate
InterfaceController, view event: WillActivate
InterfaceController, view event: DidAppear
InterfaceController, view event: WillDisappear
InterfaceController, view event: DidDeactivate
App event: ApplicationWillEnterForeground
App event: ApplicationDidBecomeActive
InterfaceController, view event: WillActivate|
```

Figure 8-9. *Application Output of the HelloWatchKit.Watch app, presenting the order of raising the view and app events by the runtime*

Text Input

Collecting user input from the wearable app is more challenging than doing so from the iOS app because watches have much smaller screens and the user typically wants to interact quickly. For this reason, WatchKit provides a dedicated text input controller that you use for gathering user input on watchOS. As shown in Figure 8-10, this controller appears as a modal window and contains a predefined list of suggested values. Additionally, depending on the controller configuration, you can collect user input as emoji, voice command, or scribble.

Figure 8-10. *Example appearance of the text input controller*

Listing 8-8. Collecting User Input with TextInputController

```
partial void ButtonInput_Activated()
{
    var colors = new string[]
    {
        "Red", "Green", "Blue", "Orange", "Purple"
    };

    PresentTextInputController(colors,
        WKTextInputMode.AllowEmoji, DisplayUserResponse);
}
```

To show how to use the text input controller, I modify the first scene defined under the HelloWatchKit. Watch app. Namely, I add a separator, a button, and a label. I set their horizontal and vertical alignment to center. Then, I change the name of the button and label to `ButtonInput` and `LabelAnswer`, respectively. Finally, I double-click the button. This creates a default event handler, `ButtonInput_Activated`, which I define as shown in Listing 8-8. In the `ButtonInput_Activated` event handler, I first create an array of strings, which serves as the list of predefined inputs or suggestions in the text input controller. Then, I show this controller to the user by invoking the `PresentTextInputController` method, which is implemented in the `WKInterfaceController` class and accepts three arguments:

- `suggestions` – an array of strings with predefined items displayed in the modal window

- `inputMode` – specifies the type of input described by one of the values declared in the `WKTextInputMode` enumeration:

  - `AllowEmojiAnimated` and `AllowEmoji` – indicate that either animated or non-animated emojis are allowed, respectively

  - `Plain` – indicates that emojis are not allowed

- `completion` – an action that is invoked after the user dismisses the controller

In Listing 8-8, I allow non-animated emojis and use a `DisplayUserResponse` action as the completion handler. As Listing 8-9 shows, the `DisplayUserResponse` method displays the first item retrieved from the text input controller and displays it in the label of name `LabelAnswer`. The text input controller returns a collection of items selected by the user as an instance of the NSArray object, which is then provided to the completion handler.

Listing 8-9. Presenting an Item Chosen by the User

```
private void DisplayUserResponse(NSArray result)
{
    var answer = "No answer";

    if (result != null)
    {
        if (result.Count > 0)
        {
            answer = result.GetItem<NSObject>(0).ToString();
        }
    }

    LabelAnswer.SetText(answer);
}
```

After re-running the app, you can press the button to activate the text input controller. It will look as previously shown in Figure 8-10. Try to tap one of the suggested values (colors) or emoji. You will see that the text input controller is dismissed and the selected value is displayed in the bottom label (Figure 8-11).

Figure 8-11. *Displaying user input gathered with text input controller*

Force Touch and Navigation

Apple Watch is equipped with the Force Touch sensor, which detects how firmly you press the screen. Force touch is also defined as an additional gesture. You can use it to extend the way your app interacts with the user. In this section, we will learn how to use the force touch to activate a menu containing a list of city names. After tapping the menu item, another interface controller will be presented. This controller will show the geolocation of the selected city (Figure 8-12).

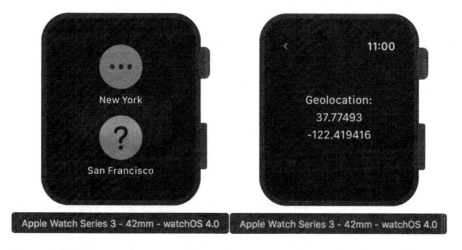

Figure 8-12. *Force touch gesture activates the menu, containing a list of cities. When you tap the item, another view is displayed. This view displays the geocoordinates of selected city.*

To implement this functionality, I open the Interface.storyboard, where I add a menu from the toolbox onto the interface controller, representing a default scene. The menu appears in the Document Outline pad under the Interface Controller item. I tap this entry, and then in the Properties pad I change the number of items from 1 to 2. Consequently, two menu items are created. To configure them, I use the Properties pad, where I set Title and Image properties under the Menu Item group as follows (Figure 8-13):

- New York and More for the first item

- San Francisco and Maybe for the second item

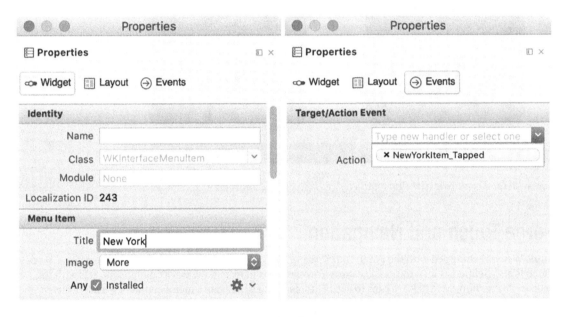

Figure 8-13. *Properties pad showing configuration of the first menu item*

Then, for each item I declare action events, which are invoked when the user taps each menu item. To that end, I use the Events tab of the Properties pad, where I type the method name and hit Enter (see right part of Figure 8-13). Visual Studio then asks me to choose a place in the code to insert an empty definition of the event handlers. I set the names of these event handlers to NewYorkItem_Tapped and SanFranciscoItem_Tapped, respectively. Before I define these event handlers, I go back to the iOS designer, where I add the new interface controller to the storyboard. Using the Properties pad of this controller, I change its class and identifier to CityGeolocationController. Then, I supplement the view of this interface controller with three labels. I center these labels vertically and horizontally and stack them as shown in Figure 8-12. Next, I set the Text property of the first label to *Geolocation:* and update the names of the two other labels to LabelLat and LabelLng.

Given the UI is now ready and configured, I can implement the logic. I start by adding a new file, LocationHelper.cs, to the HelloWatchKit.WatchExtension project. In this new file, I import the CoreLocation namespace and then define a static class, LocationHelper, and custom enumeration, City, as in Listing 8-10.

Listing 8-10. A Definition of the LocationHelper Class and Custom Enumeration City

```
public static class LocationHelper
{
    public static CLLocation GetLocationForCity(City city)
    {
        CLLocation result = null;

        switch(city)
        {
            case City.NewYork:
                result = new CLLocation(40.7127837, -74.0059413);
                break;

            case City.SanFrancisco:
            default:
                result = new CLLocation(37.77493, -122.419416);
                break;
        }

        return result;
    }
}

public enum City
{
    NewYork, SanFrancisco
}
```

LocationHelper implements a single static method, GetLocationForCity, which accepts an argument named city of type City. The latter is the enumeration defining the elements NewYork and SanFrancisco. Depending on the city argument, GetLocationForCity will return an instance of the CoreLocation. CLLocation class, which stores the geocoordinates of either New York or San Francisco. I obtained geocoordinates from the Google Geocode API.

As a next step, I open the InterfaceController.cs file, where I modify the definition of the InterfaceController class. First, I add the DisplayCityGeolocationController method seen in Listing 8-11. This method obtains geocoordinates from the LocationHelper and then passes them to the CityGeolocationController, which is initialized and presented with the PushController method. This method accepts two arguments, as follows:

- name – specifies the name of the interface controller to display

- context – optional argument you use to pass an object to the target interface controller

Here, I set the name to CityGeolocationController, and as a context I pass an instance of the CCLocation class obtained from the LocationHelper.

179

Listing 8-11. Presenting the CityGeolocationController with Geocordinates to Be Displayed

```
private void DisplayCityGeolocationController(City city)
{
    var location = LocationHelper.GetLocationForCity(city);

    PushController("CityGeolocationController", location);
}
```

Then, I use the `DisplayCityGeolocationController` method to implement event handlers associated with menu items, as shown in Listing 8-12. So, the new interface controller will be fed with different geocoordinates, depending on the user's choice.

Listing 8-12. A Context Is Passed to the CityGeolocationController

```
partial void NewYorkItem_Tapped()
{
    DisplayCityGeolocationController(City.NewYork);
}

partial void SanFranciscoItem_Tapped()
{
    DisplayCityGeolocationController(City.SanFrancisco);
}
```

Finally, I need to present geocoordinates. To that end, I modify the `CityGeolocationController.cs` file, where I first import the `CoreLocation` namespace and then modify a definition of the `CityGeolocationController` class (Listing 8-13). I supplement a default definition of this controller with a private field, `location`, two view event handlers (`Awake` and `WillActivate`), and one private method, `GetLocation`. The latter is used to obtain an instance of the `CLLocation` class from the context passed to the interface controller and store the resulting object in the `location` field. To access the context, I use the `Awake` view event handler, where I invoke the `GetLocation` method. Subsequently, when the view of the interface controller is about to be presented to the user, I change the text displayed in the labels such that they present latitude and longitude for the selected city.

To test the app, run it in the Apple Watch simulator. Then, change the touch pressure to deep press (COMMAND+SHIFT+2) and hold the screen of the simulator for a short while. This enables the menu shown previously in Figure 8-12. Now, change the touch pressure to shallow press (COMMAND+SHIFT+1) and tap one of the items. The corresponding geocoordinates will be presented (right part of Figure 8-12).

You can now easily extend this example and add a `Map` control to the view of the `CityGeolocationController`. Given the geocoordinate all you need to do is to set the map center and region just as I showed you in Chapters 3 and 7.

Listing 8-13. Presenting Latitude and Longitude

```
public partial class CityGeolocationController : WKInterfaceController
{
    private CLLocation location;

    public CityGeolocationController(IntPtr handle) : base(handle)
    {
    }
```

```
public override void Awake(NSObject context)
{
    base.Awake(context);

    GetLocation(context);
}

public override void WillActivate()
{
    LabelLat.SetText(location.Coordinate.Latitude.ToString());
    LabelLng.SetText(location.Coordinate.Longitude.ToString());
}

private void GetLocation(NSObject context)
{
    location = context as CLLocation;

    if (location == null)
    {
        location = LocationHelper.GetLocationForCity(
            City.SanFrancisco);
    }
}
}
```

Notification Controller

Notifications implement a mechanism to present new information to the user when the app is not running. Typically, remote notifications are sent to the mobile or wearable end-points from a dedicated push notification service running in the cloud. Notifications can be also sent locally. In this section, we will learn how to create a local notification in the parent iOS app. This notification will be automatically routed to the watchOS app when the iPhone is locked. Starting from iOS 10, Apple introduced a new mechanism for raising notifications. This is based on the UserNotifications API. An older API for raising local notifications (available for iOS 8 and iOS 9) is implemented within the UILocalNotification class. In this section, I will use the UserNotifications API.

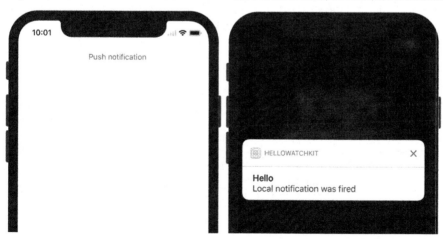

Figure 8-14. *A UI of the HelloWatchKit iOS app and local notification in the iPhone X simulator*

To raise a local notification with this API, I use the HelloWatchKit iOS project. First, I open the storyboard designer and modify the view associated with the default view controller to add a button. I open the Properties pad of this button, where I set the button's caption to *Push notification* and name to ButtonLocalNotification (Figure 8-14). Afterward, I open the Events tab to create the handler for the TouchUpInside event. Finally, I define this event handler according to Listing 8-14. This code requires me to import the UserNotifications namespace.

Listing 8-14. Pushing a Local Notification

```
partial void ButtonLocalNotification_TouchUpInside(UIButton sender)
{
    // Notification content
    var notificationContent = new UNMutableNotificationContent()
    {
        Title = "Hello",
        Body = "Local notification was fired",
    };

    // Notification will be fired after 10 seconds
    var notificationTrigger = UNTimeIntervalNotificationTrigger.
        CreateTrigger(10, false);

    // Notification request
    var notificationRequest = UNNotificationRequest.FromIdentifier(
        Guid.NewGuid().ToString(), notificationContent, notificationTrigger);

    UNUserNotificationCenter.Current.AddNotificationRequest(
        notificationRequest, null);
}
```

As shown in Listing 8-14, to create a local notification you use the UNMutableNotificationContent class. Here, I instantiate this class using a default constructor and then set the title and body of the notification using the corresponding properties of the UNMutableNotificationContent class. Subsequently, I request that the iOS fire the notification after ten seconds using UNTimeIntervalNotificationTrigger. Finally, I add the notification to the user notification center using the UNUserNotificationCenter class.

To enable your app to send local notifications, you also need to obtain user permission. To do so, I open the AppDelegate.cs file of the HelloWatchKit. Then, I import the UserNotifications namespace and modify the FinishedLaunching event handler as shown in Listing 8-15.

You can now run the HelloWatchKit app in any iPhone simulator. The app will display an alert requesting permission to send notifications. Accept this alert, then press the *Push notification* button and lock the iPhone screen. To lock the simulator, I press COMMAND+L on the keyboard. After a short while, a local notification will be presented (Figure 8-14).

Listing 8-15. Displaying a Notification in the watchOS App

```
public override bool FinishedLaunching(UIApplication application,
    NSDictionary launchOptions)
{
    UNUserNotificationCenter.Current.RequestAuthorization(
        UNAuthorizationOptions.Alert, (approved, error) => {
    });

    return true;
}
```

182

To test the notification on the watchOS simulator, I run the HelloWatchKit.Watch app. Subsequently, I go to the iPhone simulator, where I open the HelloWatchKit app. After the app is executed, I tap the *Push Notification* button and then lock the iPhone screen to ensure that the local notification will be routed to the Apple Watch. The notification will appear about ten seconds after tapping the button in the iOS app (Figure 8-15).

Figure 8-15. *A local notification received by the watchOS app*

Note that you can also execute the app such that it will present a notification controller on start. To do so, choose a corresponding item in the debug target drop-down list; for example, *HelloWatchKit. Watch – Notification.* You will quickly see the results shown in Figure 8-16. If you now open the Interface. storyboard from the HelloWatchKit.Watch bundle, you will see that the view of the notification controller does not reflect what you see on the simulator. This is because the visual appearance of the local notification is determined by the payload declared in the PushNotificationPayload.json file of the HelloWatchKit.Watch app.

Figure 8-16. *A default notification controller*

ClockKit and Complication Controller

The ClockKit is a set of classes and objects that lets you create complications. These are visual elements that appear on the watch face. Complications are somewhat similar to notifications and give the user access to important data provided by your app but in a less obstructive way than notifications. To create a complication, you use the complication controller, which was added to the Watch Extension bundle. A definition of this controller is stored in the ComplicationController.cs file. If you open this file, you will see that the ComplicationController class derives from CLKComplicationDataSource. The latter comes from the ClockKit framework and is the key ingredient in implementing the complication. Specifically, you override methods from the CLKComplicationDataSource in the derived class to control the appearance of complications. At the very least, you need to implement these methods:

- GetPlaceholderTemplate – provides a visual template for your complication. The result of this method is used by the ClockKit to present the sample appearance of the complication to the user during configuration. You typically use fake data to create such a template to give the user an idea of what your complication will look like. This method is available for watchOS 2 only.

- GetLocalizableSampleTemplate – works like GetPlaceholderTemplate with a difference being that it is used by the ClockKit to get a localizable (language-dependent) complication template. This method is available for watchOS 3 or later only.

- GetCurrentTimelineEntry – ClockKit uses this method to obtain the actual data for the complication.

- GetSupportedTimeTravelDirections – This informs the ClockKit whether your app can provide future or past data entries for the complication.

Because the preceding methods are invoked by the ClockKit, you return data to this framework through callbacks. Namely, each of these methods accepts two arguments. The first one, complication, is an instance of the CLKComplication class and is an abstract representation of the complication. The other argument, handler, is the action (callback) that you invoke to pass data for a complication. You typically use an instance of the CLKComplication class to infer the type of complication by reading its Family property. Depending on this, you perform custom logic and finally invoke a handler, in which you pass data for the ClockKit. Let's see how this works in practice. To this end, I extend the definition of the ComplicationController class from the HelloWatchKit.WatchExtension app by a method shown in Listing 8-16.

Listing 8-16. Creating a Complication Template

```
private CLKComplicationTemplate CreateComplicationTemplate(
    CLKComplicationFamily complicationFamily, string complicationText)
{
    CLKComplicationTemplate template = null;

    switch (complicationFamily)
    {
        case CLKComplicationFamily.ModularSmall:
            template = new CLKComplicationTemplateModularSmallRingText()
            {
                TextProvider = CLKSimpleTextProvider.FromText(complicationText),
                FillFraction = 0.75f,
```

```
                RingStyle = CLKComplicationRingStyle.Open
            };
            break;

        case CLKComplicationFamily.ModularLarge:
            template = new CLKComplicationTemplateModularLargeStandardBody()
            {
                HeaderTextProvider = CLKSimpleTextProvider.
                    FromText("My Complication"),
                Body1TextProvider = CLKSimpleTextProvider.
                    FromText(complicationText),
                Body2TextProvider = CLKTimeTextProvider.
                    FromDate(NSDate.Now)
            };
            break;
    }

    return template;
}
```

The first method, CreateComplicationTemplate, is used to create two complications using two separate templates—one for modular small and one for modular large complications. So, CreateComplicationTemplate accepts two arguments. The first one, complicationFamily, specifies the complication type and accepts one of the values defined in the CLKComplicationFamily enumeration. The second argument, complicationText, holds a value to be displayed in the complication.

CreateComplicationTemplate supports only two complications: modular small and modular large. To create the first one, I use CLKComplicationTemplateModularSmallRingText. This implements a visual style for the complication in which text is enclosed by a progress ring. You control the appearance of this template using the following properties of the CLKComplicationTemplateModularSmallRingText class instance:

- TextProvider – specifies a text to be displayed

- FillFraction – determines the percentage of ring to fill

- RingStyle – indicates the style of the ring, either open or closed

In Listing 8-16, I set the fill fraction to 75 percent and ring style to open. Consequently, the code from Listing 8-16 will generate the modular small complication shown in Figure 8-17.

Figure 8-17. *A fragment of the watch face depicting modular small complication*

To create the modular large complication, I utilize the CLKComplicationTemplateModular LargeStandardBody class. It can be parameterized using the following four properties:

- HeaderTextProvider – specifies text to display in the complication header

- Body1TextProvider – used to configure text displayed in the first line of body text (right below the header)

- Body2TextProvider – specifies an optional second line of body text

- HeaderImageProvider – indicates an optional image to be displayed on the left-hand side of the header

The CreateComplicationTemplate method uses the first three properties. The header displays a fixed string, My Complication, while the first and second lines depict a value obtained from the complicationText parameter and current time, respectively. An example of such a complication is presented in Figure 8-18.

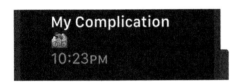

Figure 8-18. *A modular large complication*

Given the template's ready, I now extend the definition of the ComplicationController by another method, CreateComplicationEntry (Listing 8-17). It uses the previously implemented CreateComplicationTemplate to make a timeline entry with the current date.

Listing 8-17. Creating a Complication Entry

```
private CLKComplicationTimelineEntry CreateComplicationEntry(
    CLKComplicationFamily complicationFamily, string complicationText)
{
    var template = CreateComplicationTemplate(
        complicationFamily, complicationText);

    if (template != null)
    {
        return CLKComplicationTimelineEntry.Create(NSDate.Now, template);
    }
    else
    {
        return null;
    }
}
```

I now use the preceding methods to implement functions required by the ClockKit. I start with the GetPlaceholderTemplate and GetLocalizableSampleTemplate (Listing 8-18). In both methods, I first call the CreateComplicationTemplate method. Then, I pass its result, an instance of the CLKComplicationTemplate class, to the ClockKit by invoking a callback (an action handler). This conforms to the general scheme of communicating with the ClockKit I discussed earlier.

Listing 8-18. Providing Complication Templates to the ClockKit

```
public override void GetPlaceholderTemplate(CLKComplication complication,
    Action<CLKComplicationTemplate> handler)
{
    var template = CreateComplicationTemplate(
        complication.Family, "Sample text");

    handler(template);
}

public override void GetLocalizableSampleTemplate(CLKComplication complication,
    Action<CLKComplicationTemplate> handler)
{
    var template = CreateComplicationTemplate(
        complication.Family, "Sample text");

    handler(template);
}
```

Given the preceding methods are ready, I now override the GetCurrentTimelineEntry and GetSupportedTimeTravelDirections methods as shown in Listing 8-19. I disable support for the time-travel directions because I provide complications for the current date only. In the GetCurrentTimelineEntry method, I use the ComplicationHelper class, which I will discuss shortly.

Listing 8-19. Providing a Current Timeline Entry and Supported Time-Travel Directions

```
public override void GetCurrentTimelineEntry(CLKComplication complication,
    Action<CLKComplicationTimelineEntry> handler)
{
    var timelineEntry = CreateComplicationEntry(complication.Family,
        ComplicationHelper.Answer);

    handler(timelineEntry);
}

public override void GetSupportedTimeTravelDirections(
    CLKComplication complication,
    Action<CLKComplicationTimeTravelDirections> handler)
{
    handler(CLKComplicationTimeTravelDirections.None);
}
```

According to the ClockKit documentation, the use of complications is budgeted for each app to preserve system resources. When your app reaches the limit, the ClockKit will invoke RequestedUpdateBudgetExhausted. I override this method, as shown in Listing 8-20, so the information about the exhausted budget will be presented in the application output. Note that this method requires you to import the System.Diagnostics namespace.

Listing 8-20. Handling Exhaustion of the Complication Update Budget

```
public override void RequestedUpdateBudgetExhausted()
{
    Debug.WriteLine("RequestedUpdateBudgetExhausted");

    base.RequestedUpdateBudgetExhausted();
}
```

The communication between my watch extension bundle and the ClockKit is ready. So, now I need to implement a logic that will force complication updates. To that end, I use another class from the ClockKit, CLKComplicationServer. An instance of this class represents the complication server, which manages the complications and in particular can be used to update them on demand. To implement complication updates in the HelloWatchKit.WatchExtension, I add a ComplicationHelper.cs file, where I import the ClockKit namespace and then define the ComplicationHelper class, as shown in Listing 8-21.

Listing 8-21. A Definition of the ComplicationHelper

```
public static class ComplicationHelper
{
    public static string Answer { get; set; } = string.Empty;

    public static void UpdateComplications()
    {
        var server = CLKComplicationServer.SharedInstance;

        foreach (var complication in server.ActiveComplications)
        {
            server.ReloadTimeline(complication);
        }
    }
}
```

To access the complication server, you use the static property SharedInstance of the CLKComplicationServer class. Then, to obtain the collection of active complications that are actually displayed on the watch face, you read the ActiveComplications property. Each element in this collection is an instance of the CLKComplication class and gives you direct access to the complication. In particular, you can force it to be updated by passing the corresponding object to the ReloadTimeline method of the CLKComplicationServer class instance (see the UpdateComplications method in Listing 8-21). ComplicationHelper also has one static property, Answer, which I use to pass data from the interface controller to the complication controller. To finish the implementation, I need to obtain data for the complication. To this end, I modify the DisplayUserResponse method (Listing 8-9) as shown in Listing 8-22. Namely, I store the value obtained using the text input controller in the ComplicationHelper.Answer property and then force all active complications to be updated using the ComplicationHelper.UpdateComplications method.

Listing 8-22. Updating Complications

```
private void DisplayUserResponse(NSArray result)
{
    var answer = "No answer";
```

```
if (result != null)
{
    if (result.Count > 0)
    {
        answer = result.GetItem<NSObject>(0).ToString();
    }
}

LabelAnswer.SetText(answer);

ComplicationHelper.Answer = answer;
ComplicationHelper.UpdateComplications();
}
```

To test the preceding example, you need to quit the iPhone and Watch simulators and then re-run the app. Subsequently, go to the watch face, set touch pressure to deep, and tap the watch screen. This activates the mode where you can adjust the watch face. Swipe to the modular (left part of Figure 8-18) and then hit the *Customize* button after reverting the touch pressure to shallow. Once in the customization mode, swipe to the second screen and then use the green rectangle to switch between complications. Go to the complication shown in the top left corner. Subsequently, you need to place the mouse cursor on the digital crown and then scroll the mouse or touch pad until you see the HelloWatchKit.Watch complication. Do the same thing for the large complication below it (right part of Figure 8-19). Once you are done, press the digital crown button. You can now go back to the app and choose any item from the text input controller so you can see your updated complications on the home screen.

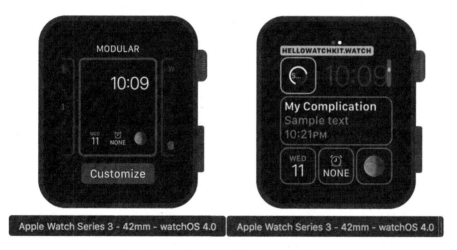

Figure 8-19. *Configuring complications*

Glance Controller

The last element of the HelloWatchKit.WatchExtension bundle is the glance controller, which is used to present static information to the user. The default glance controller was generated by Visual Studio during app creation. When the user taps the view associated with the glance controller, the corresponding app is activated. Because glances are unavailable in watchOS 3 and above, we cannot test them using default simulators. So, I will only show how to detect if the app was activated from the glance. If so, the title of the interface controller will change to the appropriate value. To implement such a functionality, I add to the HelloWatchKit.WatchExtension app another file, GlanceHelper.cs, where I define the static class seen in Listing 8-23. This class has only one property, Key, which is used to identify the value passed between the glance and interface controllers.

Listing 8-23. A Helper Class for Handling Glance Activation

```
public static class GlanceHelper
{
    public static NSString Key { get; } = new NSString("GlanceKey");
}
```

To show how to pass data from the glance to the interface controller to indicate that it was activated through the glance, I first implement the WillActivate view event handler of the GlanceController, as shown in Listing 8-24. I create the NSDictionary object, implementing the collection of key–value pairs. In this case, a dictionary contains just one element with the key GlanceKey and a value of Glance-activated. Then, I pass the dictionary along with the appIdentifier to the UpdateUserActivity method. This method is used to pass the glance state to the actual app.

Listing 8-24. Passing Data to the App When It Is Activated from the Glance Controller

```
public override void WillActivate()
{
    var appIdentifier = NSBundle.MainBundle.BundleIdentifier;

    using (var nsDictionary = new NSDictionary
        (GlanceHelper.Key, "Glance-activated"))
    {
        UpdateUserActivity(appIdentifier, nsDictionary, null);
    }
}
```

Then, to obtain the glance state, you implement HandleUserActivity in your initial interface controller. An example of how to retrieve a value for the key GlanceKey in the InterfaceController class of the HelloWatchKit.WatchExtension is shown in Listing 8-25.

Listing 8-25. Receiving Data Passed from the Glance Controller

```
public override void HandleUserActivity(NSDictionary userActivity)
{
    if (userActivity != null)
    {
        if (userActivity.ContainsKey(GlanceHelper.Key))
        {
            SetTitle(userActivity.ValueForKey(GlanceHelper.Key).ToString());
        }
    }
}
```

Summary

In this chapter, we learned how to implement apps for smartwatches. We covered a broad range of topics, starting from project creation, using the watch simulator, and handling view and app events through to collecting user input with dedicated controllers, creating force touch menus, and navigating between interface controllers up to notifications, glances, and complications. This collection of tutorials enables you to independently write complete apps for the watchOS. In the following chapter, we will work with tvOS apps.

CHAPTER 9

■ ■ ■

tvOS

TV is yet another part of everyday life that has been revolutionized by electronics and software. Devices like Apple TV turn your display into a smart device that you can use beyond just watching TV. You do not need to worry about missing your favorite TV show. Instead, you are the boss, deciding when and what you watch. Moreover, your TV becomes even more smart with dedicated apps and games. This chapter will show how to build such custom apps for Apple TV. Specifically, I will tell you how to create the complete tvOS app shown in Figure 9-1. This app will utilize the OpenWeatherMap API to display the current weather conditions for the city name you type into the text field.

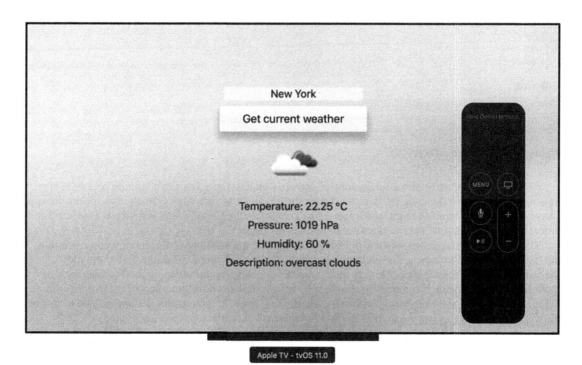

Figure 9-1. *A custom weather app for the Apple TV*

© Dawid Borycki 2018
D. Borycki, *Beginning Xamarin Development for the Mac*, https://doi.org/10.1007/978-1-4842-3132-6_9

Creating a Project

I start by creating a new tvOS project named *HelloTV*. To that end, I utilize the new Single View App from the tvOS tab of the New Project dialog in Visual Studio (Figure 9-2).

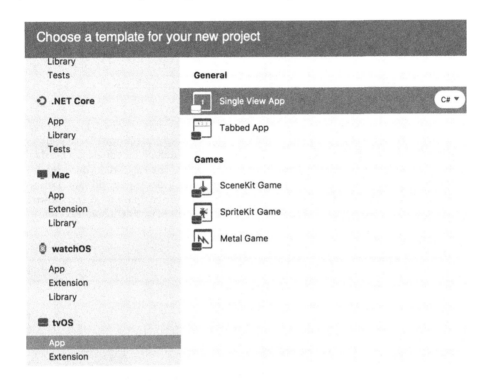

Figure 9-2. *Creating a tvOS project*

Subsequently, Visual Studio displays another screen, which is where you can configure your tvOS app. Basically, you do much the same thing as you did for the iOS and watchOS apps. Namely, you specify the app name, organization identifier, team, and target. Here, I configure the HelloTV app as shown in Figure 9-3 and proceed to the next step, where I confirm the location of my project.

Once the project is created, you will quickly recognize that the structure of the HelloTV app resembles the organization of iOS projects. The entry point of the HelloTV app is implemented within the static Main method of the Program class (Main.cs file). A default implementation of this method utilizes the AppDelegate class to launch and manage the lifecycle of the tvOS app at runtime. AppDelegate derives from UIApplicationDelegate, exactly the same one used in all iOS apps. So, you handle the app-related events of the tvOS app the same as you did in the iOS apps. For this reason, actual examples are omitted.

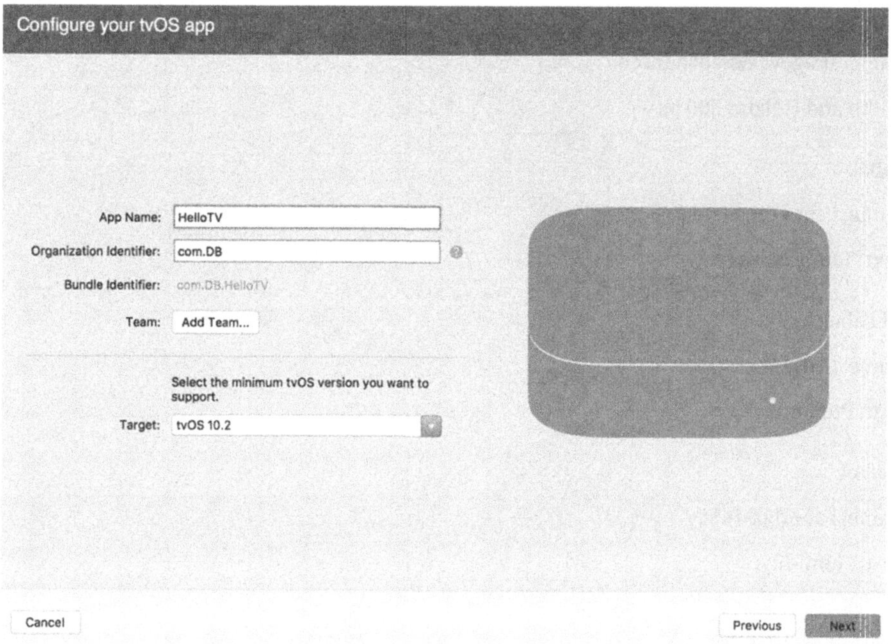

Figure 9-3. *Project configuration*

User Interface

To design the UI for the HelloTV app, I open the Solution Explorer and double-click the Main.storyboard file. This opens the iOS designer, in which I modify the scene of the default view controller. Specifically, from the toolbox I drag the following controls: a text field, a button, an image view, and four labels. As shown in Figure 9-4, I stack all the controls vertically and then use the Properties pad to configure each control as follows:

- Text Field:
  - Name: TextFieldCityName
  - Width: 500 px
  - Alignment: Center
  - Font: Headline
  - Text: Type city name

- Button:
  - Name: ButtonGetCurrentWeather
  - Width: 500 px
  - Alignment: Center
  - Font: Headline
  - Title: Get current weather

- Image View:
  - Name: ImageViewWeatherIcon
  - Width and Height: 200 px

- First Label:
  - Name: LabelTemperature
  - Text: Temperature:

- Second Label:
  - Name: LabelPressure
  - Text: Pressure:

- Third Label:
  - Name: LabelHumidity
  - Text: Humidity:

- Fourth Label:

  - Name: LabelDescription

  - Text: Description:

Additionally, I set the width, font, and alignment of all labels to 1920 px, headline, and center, respectively.

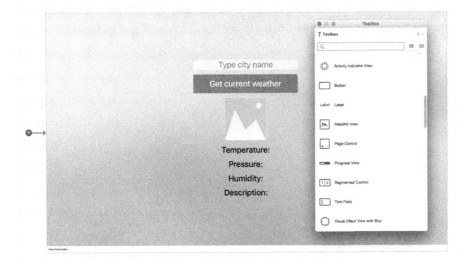

Figure 9-4. *Designing the user interface of the tvOS app*

OpenWeatherMap API

Given the UI is ready, I start implementing the logic responsible for obtaining the current weather conditions. To that end, I use the API exposed by the OpenWeatherMap web service (https://openweathermap.org/). OpenWeatherMap provides free and paid plans. The free plan is limited to 60 calls per minute (https://openweathermap.org/price) and has some other specific limitations but is more than enough to implement the HelloTV sample. To access the OpenWeatherMap API, you will need to sign up for the free account. You will receive via email your app identifier, which you use to access the REST service of OpenWeatherMap. Once this is done, you can start testing OpenWeatherMap in your browser by typing the following URL in the address bar:

```
http://api.openweathermap.org/data/2.5/weather?q=<cityname>&appid=<your app id>
```

As a result, OpenWeatherMap will return a JSON object with the structure shown in Listing 9-1. Namely, there are twelve properties, which in particular contain information about the geolocation of a weather station and report the weather conditions (coord), the actual weather conditions (weather, main, visibility, wind, clouds), and calculation date (dt).

Listing 9-1. A Sample JSON Response from the OpenWeatherMap API

```
{
  "coord": {
    "lon": -74.01,
    "lat": 40.71
  },
  "weather": [
    {
      "id": 800,
      "main": "Clear",
      "description": "clear sky",
      "icon": "01d"
    }
  ],
  "base": "stations",
  "main": {
    "temp": 290.14,
    "pressure": 1016,
    "humidity": 77,
    "temp_min": 287.15,
    "temp_max": 292.15
  },
  "visibility": 16093,
  "wind": {
    "speed": 2.92,
    "deg": 272.003
  },
  "clouds": {
    "all": 1
  },
  "dt": 1504527300,
  "sys": {
    "type": 1,
    "id": 1969,
```

```
      "message": 0.0186,
      "country": "US",
      "sunrise": 1504520803,
      "sunset": 1504567326
    },
    "id": 5128581,
    "name": "New York",
    "cod": 200
}
```

To consume the preceding JSON response in the HelloTV app, I need to map the JSON object to the C# classes. As in Chapter 7, I do this mapping with the help of the JSON Utils service (https://jsonutils.com/). In particular, I paste the JSON response into the JSON Test or URL text field, set the class name to WeatherInfo, check "Pascal Case," and click the *Submit* button. Consequently, a set of classes is generated. I save all of these classes in separate files under the Models folder of the HelloTV app (see companion code: Chapter_09/HelloTV/Models).

A detailed description of each autogenerated class is not warranted. So, I will describe the most important elements only. The main class representing the top-level properties of the JSON response is WeatherInfo. The definition of this class appears in Listing 9-2. Accordingly, WeatherInfo contains twelve autogenerated properties, which you can use to read weather conditions.

Listing 9-2. A Definition of the WeatherInfo Class

```
public class WeatherInfo
{
    public Coord Coord { get; set; }
    public IList<Weather> Weather { get; set; }
    public string Base { get; set; }
    public Main Main { get; set; }
    public int Visibility { get; set; }
    public Wind Wind { get; set; }
    public Clouds Clouds { get; set; }
    public int Dt { get; set; }
    public Sys Sys { get; set; }
    public int Id { get; set; }
    public string Name { get; set; }
    public int Cod { get; set; }
}
```

In particular, in the HelloTV app I use only two properties of the WeatherInfo class instance: Main and Weather. The first one stores the temperature, pressure, and humidity (Listing 9-3). These values will then be displayed in corresponding labels of the UI. An instance of the Main class also has two other properties: TempMin and TempMax. You can use them to obtain the minimum and maximum temperatures. They indicate a deviation from the current temperature, which according to the OpenWeatherMap documentation can appear for large cities. The second element of the WeatherInfo class I will use is the collection called Weather. Each element of this collection is an instance of the Weather class (Listing 9-4). A Weather class has four properties:

- Id – represents an identifier of the element in the collection

- Main – group of weather parameters

- Description – text description of current weather conditions

- Icon – an identifier of the icon that graphically illustrates the weather

In the HelloTV app, I use the last two; a description is displayed in the last label, while the icon identifier is used to create an image displayed right above the temperature (refer back to Figure 9-1). I will tell you how I get this image.

Listing 9-3. Main Object Stores the Temperature, Pressure, and Humidity Readings

```
public class Main
{
    public double Temp { get; set; }
    public double Pressure { get; set; }
    public double Humidity { get; set; }
    public double TempMin { get; set; }
    public double TempMax { get; set; }
}
```

Listing 9-4. A Weather Object Stores Description and Icon Identifier

```
public class Weather
{
    public int Id { get; set; }
    public string Main { get; set; }
    public string Description { get; set; }
    public string Icon { get; set; }
}
```

Retrieving the Weather Report

Given an established mapping between JSON and the C# objects, I proceed to implement the class that sends HTTP GET requests to the OpenWeatherMap API. This class, WeatherServiceHelper (see Helpers subfolder of the HelloTV app in the companion code), uses an HttpClient object, which I explained in Chapter 7. To use the HttpClient class in the HelloTV project, I reference the System.Net.dll and then install the Newtonsoft.JSON NuGet package. Subsequently, I implement the class constructor to instantiate the HttpClient, with the BaseAddress property pointing to the OpenWeatherMap URL (Listing 9-5).

Listing 9-5. Creating the HTTP Client for the OpenWeatherMap API

```
private static HttpClient httpClient;

static WeatherServiceHelper()
{
    httpClient = new HttpClient()
    {
        BaseAddress = new Uri("http://api.openweathermap.org/data/2.5/weather")
    };
}
```

After configuring the HTTP client, I can start sending weather requests. To do so, in the WeatherServiceHelper I implement the static asynchronous method GetWeatherInfo (Listing 9-6). This method accepts two arguments. The first one stores the city name, while the second defines the units in which OpenWeatherMap returns weather conditions. Clearly, OpenWeatherMap can return the temperature using different scales: Kelvin, Celsius, or Fahrenheit. To specify the scale, you use one of the values that I defined in the custom enumeration type, TemperatureUnit (see the Enums\TemperatureUnit.cs file of the HelloTV app):

- Default – indicates that default units shall be used. In that case, the temperature is expressed in Kelvins (see Listing 9-1, for example).

- Metric – instructs the OpenWeatherMap API to use metric units, which means that temperature will be given in degrees Celsius

- Imperial – represents imperial units, in which temperature is expressed in degrees Fahrenheit

The values you pass to the GetWeatherInfo method are then used to create the Uniform Resource Identifier (URI) of the request (Listing 9-7). This request is then sent to the OpenWeatherMap API. After the response is received, I analyze its status code (CheckStatusCode method). Similarly, as in Chapter 7, I raise an exception when the status code differs from 200 (OK). Otherwise, I convert the response body to JSON format and deserialize it with the JsonConvert class.

Listing 9-6. Getting the Weather Info

```
public static async Task<WeatherInfo> GetWeatherInfo(
    string cityName, TemperatureUnit unit)
{
    var getRequestUri = GetRequestUri(cityName, unit);
    var response = await httpClient.GetAsync(getRequestUri);

    CheckStatusCode(response.StatusCode);

    var jsonString = await response.Content.ReadAsStringAsync();

    return JsonConvert.DeserializeObject<WeatherInfo>(jsonString);
}

private static void CheckStatusCode(HttpStatusCode statusCode)
{
    if (statusCode != HttpStatusCode.OK)
    {
        throw new Exception($"Unexpected status code: {statusCode}");
    }
}
```

Constructing the request URI imposes additional comments. As Listing 9-7 shows, I supplement the base address with a query string containing three parameters:

- appId – used to authenticate the request with the identifier obtained from the OpenWeatherMap service

- q – indicates the city or location for which weather conditions should be returned

- units – specify units

The value for the first parameter is obtained from the private field appId (Listing 9-7), so you need to update this field to the value you obtained during registration for the OpenWeatherMap service. Other query string parameters are achieved from the GetRequestUri function parameters. Note that to specify units I use TemperatureUnit enumeration. To convert values of this type to actual query string parameters, I wrote a helper method, TemperatureUnitToQueryString, shown in Listing 9-8.

Listing 9-7. Preparing the Request URI

```
private static string appId = "<type your app id here>";

private static string GetRequestUri(string cityName, TemperatureUnit unit)
{
    return $"?appId={appId}"
        + $"&q={cityName}"
        + $"&{TemperatureUnitToQueryString(unit)}";
}
```

Listing 9-8. Creating Units Query String Parameter

```
private static string TemperatureUnitToQueryString(TemperatureUnit unit)
{
    var queryString = "units=";

    switch(unit)
    {
        case TemperatureUnit.Imperial:
            queryString += "imperial";
            break;

        case TemperatureUnit.Metric:
            queryString += "metric";
            break;
    }

    return queryString;
}
```

The very last element of the WeatherServiceHelper class is the GetTemperatureUnitString method. It determines the textual representation of the unit in which temperature is expressed. For imperial and metric units, I use °F and °C, respectively, while for default scale I use the K symbol (Listing 9-9).

Listing 9-9. Obtaining Symbols Representing Temperature Scale

```
public static string GetTemperatureUnitString(TemperatureUnit unit)
{
    var unitString = string.Empty;
    var degSymbol = (char)176;

    switch (unit)
    {
        case TemperatureUnit.Imperial:
            unitString = $"{degSymbol}F";
            break;

        case TemperatureUnit.Metric:
            unitString = $"{degSymbol}C";
            break;
```

```
        case TemperatureUnit.Default:
        default:
            unitString = "K";
            break;
    }

    return unitString;
}
```

Presenting the Weather

We now have everything prepared to get and display the weather conditions, so let's combine the UI layer with the WeatherServiceHelper. To achieve this functionality, I implement the ViewController class. First, I define the DisplayWeatherInfo method, shown in Listing 9-10. This method takes an instance of the WeatherInfo class (weatherInfo argument) and displays the values of its selected properties in the default view. It is also possible to pass a null for the weatherInfo argument. In such cases, DisplayWeatherInfo displays alternate symbols (--) instead of the actual values of the temperature, humidity, pressure, and description.

Listing 9-10. Displaying Weather Conditions

```
private async Task DisplayWeatherInfo(WeatherInfo weatherInfo)
{
    var alternateSymbol = "--";
    var tempUnit = WeatherServiceHelper.GetTemperatureUnitString(
        temperatureUnit);
    var pressureUnit = "hPa";

    if(weatherInfo == null)
    {
        LabelTemperature.Text = $"Temperature: {alternateSymbol}";
        LabelHumidity.Text = $"Humidity: {alternateSymbol}";
        LabelPressure.Text = $"Pressure: {alternateSymbol}";
        LabelDescription.Text = $"Description: {alternateSymbol}";
    }
    else
    {
        LabelTemperature.Text = "Temperature: "
            + $"{weatherInfo.Main.Temp} {tempUnit}";
        LabelHumidity.Text = "Humidity: "
            + $"{weatherInfo.Main.Humidity} %";
        LabelPressure.Text = "Pressure: "
            + $"{weatherInfo.Main.Pressure} {pressureUnit}";
        LabelDescription.Text = "Description: "
            + $"{weatherInfo.Weather.FirstOrDefault().Description}";
        ImageViewWeatherIcon.Image = await IconHelper.GetIcon(weatherInfo);
    }
}
```

Displaying text in labels is straightforward. I just rewrite the properties of the WeatherInfo class instance to the Text property of the label. To display an icon, a little bit more effort is necessary. The OpenWeatherMap API returns icon identifiers, which you can use to get the URLs of the actual bitmaps in PNG format. The general structure of such a URL is the following:

```
http://openweathermap.org/img/w/<iconId>.png
```

where the <iconId> is the value you obtain when you request that the OpenWeatherMap API provides the current weather conditions for the selected city. The icon identifier is stored in the Icon property of the Weather object.

Once given the icon URL, I must download the icon and then convert it to an instance of the UIImage class so it can be displayed in the Image View control. To implement such a functionality, I add to the HelloTV project the IconHelper class (see IconHelper.cs file under the Helpers folder). A full definition of the IconHelper class appears in Listing 9-11. As shown there, the IconHelper has three private static fields: httpClient, baseAddress, and iconExtension. The first one stores a reference to the HttpClient class instance, which is used to actually download a byte array representing the bitmap from the OpenWeatherMap service. The second one, baseAddress, stores the main part of the URL from which the icons are retrieved, and the last one, iconExtension, is a constant storing the .png extension. The values retrieved from baseAddress and iconExtension—along with the icon identifier obtained from the WeatherInfo class instance—are combined into the final URL (see the GetIconUrl method in Listing 9-11). The resulting URL is then used in the GetIcon method, where I pass that URL as an argument of the GetByteArrayAsync method of the HttpClient class instance. GetByteArrayAsync returns an array of bytes representing the image data, which I use to instantiate the UIImage class with the LoadFromData static method (last statement of the GetIcon method in Listing 9-11). Note that to convert an array of bytes returned by the GetByteArrayAsync to an NSData object accepted by UIImage.LoadFromData, I must use the FromArray static method of the NSData class.

Listing 9-11. Definition of the IconHelper Class

```
public static class IconHelper
{
    private static HttpClient httpClient;

    private static string baseAddress = "http://openweathermap.org/img/w/";
    private static string iconExtension = ".png";

    static IconHelper()
    {
        httpClient = new HttpClient();
    }

    public static async Task<UIImage> GetIcon(WeatherInfo weatherInfo)
    {
        var iconUrl = GetIconUrl(weatherInfo);

        var imageData = await httpClient.GetByteArrayAsync(iconUrl);

        return UIImage.LoadFromData(NSData.FromArray(imageData));
    }
```

```
    private static string GetIconUrl(WeatherInfo weatherInfo)
    {
        var iconName = weatherInfo.Weather.FirstOrDefault().Icon;

        return $"{baseAddress}{iconName}{iconExtension}";
    }
}
```

Afterward, I invoke DisplayWeatherInfo with a null argument within the ViewDidLoad event handler (Listing 9-12). This is done to set the Text properties of all labels to initial values. In the ViewDidLoad event handler, I also wire the ButtonGetCurrentWeather_PrimaryActionTriggered method with the PrimaryActionTriggered event of the button. This action is raised when the user taps the button.

Listing 9-12. Configuring a View

```
public async override void ViewDidLoad()
{
    base.ViewDidLoad();

    await DisplayWeatherInfo(null);

    ButtonGetCurrentWeather.PrimaryActionTriggered
        += ButtonGetCurrentWeather_PrimaryActionTriggered;
}
```

Listing 9-13 shows a definition of the ButtonGetCurrentWeather_PrimaryActionTriggered method. This function works as follows. When the user taps the button, I first read the city name that he or she entered into the text field. If the city name is empty, I display the modal window with the following message, *Please enter the city name*. To display an alert, I wrote the DisplayOkAlert method. As Listing 9-14 shows, this method employs the same classes (UIAlrtController and UIAlertAction) as we used previously to display alerts in iOS apps. However, the alert window looks different (see Figure 9-5).

Listing 9-13. Retrieving and Displaying Weather Conditions

```
private TemperatureUnit temperatureUnit = TemperatureUnit.Metric;

private async void ButtonGetCurrentWeather_PrimaryActionTriggered(
    object sender, EventArgs e)
{
    var cityName = TextFieldCityName.Text;

    if(string.IsNullOrEmpty(cityName))
    {
        DisplayOkAlert("Please enter the city name");
    }
    else
    {
        try
        {
            var weatherInfo = await WeatherServiceHelper.GetWeatherInfo(
                cityName, temperatureUnit);
```

```
        await DisplayWeatherInfo(weatherInfo);
    }
    catch(Exception ex)
    {
        DisplayOkAlert(ex.Message);
    }
  }
}
```

Figure 9-5. *Although tvOS uses the same classes to display alerts as iOS, appropriate tvOS windows look differently (refer back to Chapter 1).*

Listing 9-14. Presenting an Alert

```
private void DisplayOkAlert(string message)
{
    var controller = UIAlertController.Create(
        "HelloTV", message, UIAlertControllerStyle.Alert);

    var okAction = UIAlertAction.Create(
        "OK", UIAlertActionStyle.Default, null);

    controller.AddAction(okAction);

    PresentViewController(controller, true, null);
}
```

If the user provides a valid city name, ButtonGetCurrentWeather_PrimaryActionTriggered sends a request to the OpenWeatherMap API using the WeatherServiceHelper.GetWeatherInfo method. This function returns an instance of the WeatherInfo class, which is afterward passed to the DisplayWeatherInfo method to update the UI with the received weather conditions.

Temperature Units

To specify units in the ViewController class, I declared a private field, temperatureUnit. Its default value is set to TemperatureUnit.Metric. Therefore, when you run the app it displays temperature in degree Celsius. To get temperature readings in a different scale you need to change the value of the temperatureUnit field. For instance, if you change it to TemperatureUnit.Imperial you will get results similar to those presented in Figure 9-6.

Figure 9-6. *Presenting weather conditions with imperial units (compare with Figure 9-1)*

Testing the App in a Simulator

To test the HelloTV app, you can use a simulator. To launch the app, you proceed similarly to in previous chapters. Just use the Target/Debug pad to set the app to HelloTV, pick the Apple TV tvOS 11.0 simulator, and then run the app. After a short while, you will see the app running in the simulator (Figure 9-7). The app displays a text field, button, and four labels with alternate symbols. You will also note that you cannot directly click or tap any visual control with the mouse or a touchpad. Instead, to control the simulator, you use either the Apple TV Remote or the keyboard of the Mac you use for development.

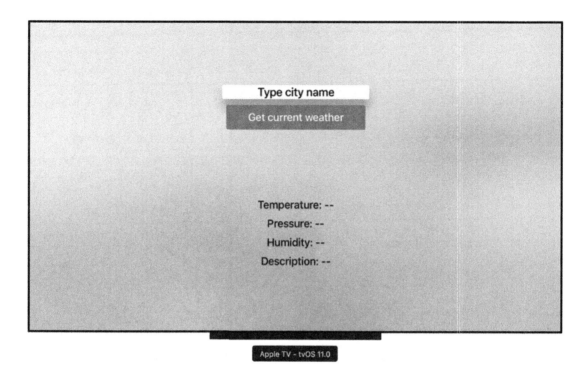

Figure 9-7. A default view of the HelloTV app right after the app is launched in the tvOS simulator

To enable both options, you use the Hardware menu of the simulator. Go to Hardware ➤ Show Apple TV Remote to activate the remote control, or ensure that the following option—Hardware ➤ Keyboard ➤ Connect Hardware Keyboard—is on (to use the keyboard). Once the remote control is enabled, you use its pad to move the cursor within the screen of the simulator. To tap any control, you press the ALT/OPTION key and then tap the virtual controller's pad. If you want to use the keyboard, then you navigate between controls using arrows. Use the Enter key to perform an action and the ESC key to get back from a menu or to dismiss windows. You will see that once you navigate between visual items they become highlighted.

Now, whichever method you choose, tap the text field. This activates the window in which you can type the city name (Figure 9-8). Replace the default value with a city name and confirm your selection by pressing the *Done* button. After getting back to the main view of the HelloTV app, press the *Get current weather* button. An app displays values obtained from the OpenWeatherMap API, as shown in Figure 9-9.

Figure 9-8. *A default tvOS screen you use to enter text into a text field*

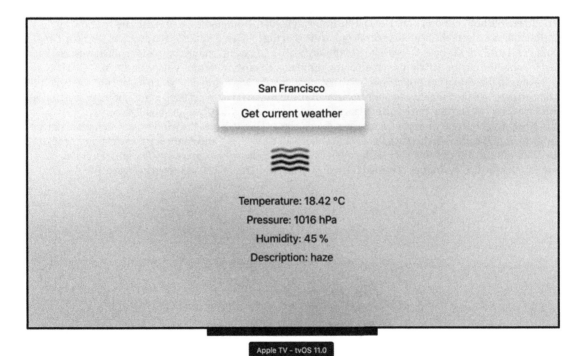

Figure 9-9. *Current weather in San Francisco obtained with the HelloTV app*

Summary

In this chapter, we learned how to start implementing apps for tvOS. Using the OpenWeatherMap API, I showed you how to develop an app that presents the weather conditions for the selected city. You can easily extend this functionality to display the weather forecast. To that end, you will need to modify the base address of the request such that `weather` is replaced by `forecast`. Afterward, map the JSON response to the appropriate C# objects and display their properties in the UI. To display a forecast, you might consider using different controls, like the Table View. It will be a good exercise for you to practice the knowledge you learned in this and all previous chapters.

This chapter also ends the book. I hope you enjoyed all the content, and I am more than sure that the presented material will help you jumpstart developing mobile apps for iOS, watchOS, and tvOS. Although I did not cover many advanced features of each platform, you should be able to use these features with the help of the Apple SDK documentation because, as I explained in Chapter 2, the corresponding API is mapped by Xamarin.iOS to C# classes and interfaces. So, I wish you good luck in your development and am looking forward to seeing your apps in the Apple Store.

Index

© Dawid Borycki 2018
D. Borycki, *Beginning Xamarin Development for the Mac*, https://doi.org/10.1007/978-1-4842-3132-6

Get the eBook for only $5!

Why limit yourself?

With most of our titles available in both PDF and ePUB format, you can access your content wherever and however you wish—on your PC, phone, tablet, or reader.

Since you've purchased this print book, we are happy to offer you the eBook for just $5.

To learn more, go to http://www.apress.com/companion or contact support@apress.com.

Apress®

Printed in the United States
By Bookmasters